Ms. Communication

Seven Keys
to Speak Your Mind Without Losing It

Ms. Communication

Seven Keys
to Speak Your Mind Without Losing It

Crista F. Benavídez

Copyright © 2019 by Crista F. Benavídez. All rights reserved. No part of this book may be used or reproduced in any manner whatsoever without written permission except in the case of brief quotations included in critical articles and reviews. For information, address Permissions@CitrinePublishing.com. To contact the author, visit www.ChispasPerformanceSolutions.com.

Limit of Liability/Disclaimer of Warranty: While the publisher and author have used their best efforts in preparing this book, they make no representations or warranties with respect to the accuracy or completeness of the contents of this book and specifically disclaim any implied warranties of merchantability or fitness for a particular purpose. The author of this book does not dispense medical advice or prescribe the use of any technique as a form of treatment for physical, emotional, or medical problems without the advice of a physician. The intent of the author is only to offer information of a general nature to help you in your quest for well-being. In the event you use any of the information in the book for yourself, which is your constitutional right, the author and publisher assume no responsibility for your actions. The views expressed in this work are solely those of the author and do not necessarily reflect the views of the the publisher.

Cover Design: Kennedy Williams • Cover Photo: Christopher T. Barber • Interior Photo: Deanna Vincent, Dry Heat Photography • Definitions sourced from Merriam-Webster.com

Library of Congress Cataloging-in-Publication Data

Benavídez, Crista F.
Ms. Communication: Seven Keys to Speak Your Mind Without Losing It

p. cm.
Paperback ISBN: 978-1-947708-39-6
Hardcover ISBN: 978-1-947708-40-2
Ebook ISBN: 978-1-947708-42-6
Library of Congress Control Number: 2019919918
First Edition, December 2019

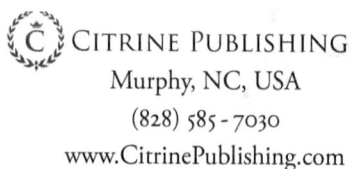

CITRINE PUBLISHING
Murphy, NC, USA
(828) 585-7030
www.CitrinePublishing.com

Praise for
Ms. Communication

"*Ms. Communication* honors the woman who never felt like she had a voice important enough to be heard. After you read this book, your communication weaknesses will become a story of your past and your future self will speak with power. Crista F. Benavídez is destined to help women around the world express themselves with truth. Allow one of them to be you."

—**Antthony Mark Hankins,** *Fashion Designer*
Antthony Design Originals

"No matter where you are in your career—or your life—I highly urge you to not just read this book, but USE this book for the accessible and authentic toolkit that it is. Crista's writing is personal, heartfelt and concise; you will quickly fall into her words as if you've plopped yourself down on the couch with a dear friend who happens to be a seasoned personal coach. She has provided powerful, useful reminders (or eye-openers) to trust yourself and to find your authority with poise, clarity and confidence; this will be mandatory reading in my own house and in my organization."

—**Tessah Latson,** *Director*
Barelas Economic Opportunity Center (BEOC)
Albuquerque Hispano Chamber of Commerce

Praise for
Ms. Communication

"Crista F. Benavídez is a communication expert! In *Ms. Communication*, she gives her readers the tools they need to be an effective communicator in their professional and their personal lives. Plus, she shares secrets gleaned throughout her career to show you exactly what to say, how to finesse your speech, and how to get the results you desire. All of this wisdom applies to the written word, too. If you are ready to be a masterful communicator, then this book is for you!"

—**Ursula Mentjes**, *Speaker, Entrepreneur, and Award-Winning Author of* The Belief Zone

"*In Ms. Communication*, Crista F. Benavídez makes it easy to understand common problems that occur when we do not express ourselves clearly—'Keep It Simple.' Communication is one of the most important life skills; this easy, enjoyable read walks its talk with profound and clear reminders of the basic communication techniques that we all sometimes forget and benefit from exponentially when we remember. I highly recommend this book!"

—**Yeseñia Ramirez**, *Vice President of Public Relations, R5 Energy Services*

Para Mimis y Babes
For Mimis and Babes

Contents

	Acknowledgments	*xi*
	Introduction	*xv*
1	Key Number One **LISTEN**	1
2	Key Number Two **PROJECT CONFIDENCE**	29
3	Key Number Three **KEEP IT SIMPLE**	53
4	Key Number Four **LEVERAGE THE POWER OF "I"**	77
5	Key Number Five **OWN IT**	99
6	Key Number Six **DECIDE**	115
7	Key Number Seven **REFLECT AND CELEBRATE**	129
8	CONCLUSION **COMMUNICATION CAN BE COMPLEX BECAUSE WE ARE**	139
	About the Author	*149*
	Take Action!	*152*

Acknowledgments

Thank you to everyone who helped me bring this book to life.

First and foremost, I thank God. To say that He guided me is an understatement. With God, all things are possible. To Him, I give the glory.

Kerry Lindberg, thank you for hosting and inviting me to the tea party that allowed me to hear God's message that it was time for me to write this book. I am forever grateful for your friendship and never-failing faith.

Gloria Hawker, I appreciate you dearly for sharing your experience and expertise with how to select an editor and navigate the publishing process. Your offer to be one of the first readers of my manuscript was just the boost of confidence I needed to move from idea, to outline, to completed manuscript.

Phillip Herndon, Bernadette Jaramillo, Melissa "Mel" Vigil, Randy Asselin, Monica Frésquez, Farid Khoury, Luis Galarza, Jacqueline Costello, and Nicole Casanova. Whether you knew it or not, my time and private conversations with each of you enabled me to "speak my mind without losing it" and remove the clutter of self-defeating thoughts that might have kept me from becoming an author. Thank you for your time, your prayers, your support, and your friendship.

Ursula Mentjes, when I told you that I felt called to write a book, you could have responded by saying that I could write the book after I made more sales calls and booked more clients. Instead, you congratulated me and said you would assist me however you could. And you did. Thank you for your encouragement and for introducing me to Amanda Johnson, my/our editor at True to Intention.

Amanda, you were a delight to work with and made the editing process so easy and efficient. Thank you for helping me bring all the client stories to life!

Kennedy Williams at Bluecoat Marketing. I came to you with only the outline for the book and a few ideas for what I wanted in a book cover, and you nailed it! You are a rock star designer who I am also grateful to call my friend. ¡Muchisimas gracias!

Christopher Martinez at Nativo Design. Thank you for taking my ideas for the keys at the beginning of each chapter from concept to completed design. They look amazing and are exactly what I envisioned.

To my group of pre-readers—John Lee Bingham, Monica Frésquez, Luis Galarza, Gloria Hawker, Marti Murphy, Ursula Mentjes, Page Ollice, and Sylvia Adamsko. I greatly appreciate the time you took to read my manuscript and share your honest feedback. Thankfully, I was able to write something that you all enjoyed reading as you supported its metamorphosis from manuscript to published book.

Last, and certainly not least, my publisher, Penelope Love, at Citrine Publishing. You were the *key* I was searching for to bring my vision for

Ms. Communication to fruition. Your caring professionalism and collaborative approach to getting her published made the process stress-free and exciting. ¡*Mil gracias!*

Introduction

I screeched to a halt when I saw her animal-print high heels firmly planted in my path as I walked toward the back of the hotel ballroom where I was facilitating a class for hard-working and dedicated administrative professionals.

Met by the scowling face of a petite, short-haired, middle-aged woman, I looked her straight in the eyes just before she started in on me: "Crista, you have just wasted two hours of my time talking about your nephew…" Her speed picked up as she listed her complaints and demands, simultaneously overwhelming my nose with the smell of cigarettes.

What in the…? I wondered while listening to everything she was saying, and feeling the eyes and ears of dozens of other people on me.

She has some nerve, calling me out in front of other people. And everything she just said is not true! First, the seminar started at 9:00 a.m. and it is only 10:15 a.m. Two hours have not elapsed. Second, the story about my nephew was only five minutes long and I know that for sure because I timed it. Finally, I am not responsible for her experience or able to refund her money.

I stayed silent for a moment that felt like hours. My heart was racing almost as fast as she was talking and my blood was beginning to boil when finally she blurted, "I would like my money back right now before I leave." She folded her arms for emphasis.

Seventy-nine sets of eyes and ears waited for me to respond. This was my moment of truth. What kind of woman was I going to be? Was I going to cry and bite my tongue? Or was I going to stand up for myself and stand my ground with the new words, phrases, and composure I had been developing and practicing in my head over the previous year?

Was I going to speak my mind effectively or totally lose it? It was a split-second decision.

Have you ever been in a situation like this, or had a conversation with someone, only to think of the perfect thing you could have said *after* the conversation was over? Having the right words at the right moment seems to come easily to other people but not to you. This is one reason why you have decided to read this book. Not to mention, lack of confidence in being able to express yourself effectively is costing you time, energy, money, and sanity.

To say that *I have been learning how to speak my mind without losing it my entire life* is not an exaggeration. As the daughter of retired teachers (Dad taught English and Social Studies while Mom taught Head Start, Kindergarten, Home Economics, Culinary Arts, Applied Math, and Marriage and Parenting), I learned from an early age that speaking well was *very* important and expected. While I developed skill with the mechanics of speaking, the only thing I learned about the emotional aspects of speaking was how to "not be so emotional." Sound familiar?

It is one thing to say what is on your mind while addressing the technical aspects of speaking, like proper diction, pronunciation, grammar, vocabulary, volume, breath control, etc. But what about the non-technical aspects, like feeling good, genuine, real, honest, confident, happy, angry, passionate, disappointed, etc., *while* you are speaking? Are these aspects not important? Indeed they are.

Unfortunately, if you have not learned to give both the technical and the emotional elements of your speaking voice time and attention, your verbal messages are likely imbalanced and not as effective as they could be. Whether you are the more technical communicator or the more emotional communicator, this book is for you. In the following chapters, I will guide you through the Seven Keys to Speak Your Mind Without Losing It.

Since 1999, I have been self-employed as a professional speaker and trainer, designing and delivering presentations and classes to help people like you achieve their personal and professional development goals; but my experience with public speaking began when I decided to run for president of the junior high student council in seventh grade. I wrote and presented my first speech to approximately 125 junior high school students and a handful of teachers. And I won the election! After this success, I went on to author and present other speeches as I ran for offices at the local and state level in academics and vocational student organizations. While I was seemingly "a natural" at speaking in public, I had challenges with one-on-one interactions. I have never considered myself shy, but definitely reserved. The most difficult situations were the one-on-one conversations with a teacher or Mom or Dad while they provided me with feedback. I often felt "put on the spot." Even when the feedback was constructive, I regularly became defensive and would shut down, bite my tongue and say nothing or, worse, begin crying. I hated the fact that I was not able to express myself effectively in all circumstances. How could I be *so* poised and confident in front of audiences as large as 3,000 yet lose it in front of one person?

This defensiveness, shutting down, and crying followed me into adulthood until about age twenty-six when it occurred to me that I had not approached my personal interactions the same way I had tackled my public presentations. After all, before I ever went on stage or into a competition, I practiced. I gave myself pep talks. Teachers, professors, and coaches recorded me and pointed out what was working and what was not. As a result, I was prepared. I never prepared for, nor had I been coached on, personal interactions.

So what changed when I was twenty-six? That is when I left my job in telecommunications to pursue my dream of becoming a professional speaker.

My first contract was with a one-day seminar company. I learned quickly that if I was going to earn a living, I not only needed to be a proficient seminar leader/teacher, I also needed to learn all about the content and resources I would be selling at the back of the room every time I delivered a seminar. How better to learn about them than to check them out, right? I took in as many books and seminars I could, both at home and while I was traveling to deliver the seminars. What started out as simply wanting to know enough about the resources so that I could sell them turned into my school-of-life degrees on subjects like diffusing anger and communicating assertively, emotional control, self-discipline, psychology, achievement, winning, and many more. These courses gave me the information and guidance I needed to become a more balanced communicator, adding the emotional piece that I had been missing. I wrote this book to share with you stories of growth and the lessons I've learned through working with people building these skills, and as I've built them myself.

Before I introduce you to the Seven Keys to Speak Your Mind Without Losing It, here are a few things I want you to know about this book. First, because I have successfully delivered nearly 2,000 seminars and presentations, I decided that I wanted to write it as if I were speaking to you in person. Participants over the years have thanked me for being down to earth, dynamic, and real, so I'm going to give it to you straight. In every chapter, I offer **Reflections** for you to think about. Take the time to do each of these before moving forward. They only take a minute or two and will help you get the most out of this book. In addition, I share real stories of women who have attempted and sometimes failed to use (and, in some cases, successfully used) the keys I am discussing. To preserve their privacy, they are identified by initials only. Each one's story may well be your story. I share them with you so that you know that you are not alone. You are not the only one who has struggled or succeeded with speaking your mind. There is strength in our weaknesses as long as we grow from them. There is also strength in celebrating our sucesses rather than taking them for granted.

The middle-aged lady waited tapping her animal-print high heels, arms crossed and lips pursed, while I strategically took a silent deep breath, strengthened my stance by moving my right foot forward slightly, and said, "Sharon, thank you for sharing your feedback. Please tell me, what specifically did you want to take away from this seminar?"

With elevated volume and speed, she quickly responded, "I came to learn about time management and you have wasted my time! I want my money back so I can leave!" By this point, she was shaking and speaking through clenched teeth.

With both self-control and a sense of urgency, I swiftly explained, "Sharon, as I stated in the introduction, time management is a topic I cover after lunch. I am willing to give you an overview right now before you leave so that you can have the information you want. As far as the refund, I am happy to give you the number for customer service. Only they can give you a refund. There are phones in the lobby that you may use to call them. I would like to give you more than just the time-management information. Would you consider staying for more of the seminar? Or would you like me to give you an overview of time management right now?"

Suddenly, mouth gaping and wide-eyed, she stammered, "Uh, oh, well, I don't know!" before spinning around and walking away.

I felt all the eyes and ears quickly turn away from us and the talking resumed while I quickly made my way to the back of the room. There was a line of people waiting for me. My registration assistant and I hustled to help everyone as best as we could in the remaining ten minutes of the break.

When it was time to resume the seminar, I noticed that Sharon had returned and I was surprised when she stayed for the entire program. I also noticed she only left after purchasing approximately $300 in resources.

The new me won! I congratulated myself as I watched her walk out of the ballroom with a smile on her face. It was like an out-of-body experience.

That could have gone sooooo wrong, I thought as I drove to the next seminar. *The old me would have been fighting back tears from feeling embarrassed and criticized. The old me would have wanted to defend myself and point out every place she had spoken inaccurately.*

I laughed to myself as I imagined some hot-blooded, take-no-bullsh*t, street Latina version of me getting in her petite, cigarette-breathing face and telling her that she was messing with the wrong person and how dare she call me out in front of other people with lies and disrespect.

Yeah, I could have totally lost it!

It is possible to become a balanced, powerful, and effective Ms. Communicator—to truly speak your mind without losing it. I am proof. I have taken the steps, I have learned how, and I continue to practice doing it every day. I am not, however, nor will I ever be, a perfect communicator because perfection is impossible. And truly, many of my most powerful lessons have come from communicating the wrong way. As you practice what you learn here, remember that I am with you every step of the way. Know that you are on the right track and that "even if you're on the right track, you're going to get run over if you just sit there!" as Will Rogers once said.

Commit to taking action and implementing what you learn in each chapter. As you begin to process this information and consider the reflections throughout this book, reward yourself with kindness, compassion, and love. That which gets rewarded, gets repeated.

Then, go one step beyond and share it with someone else.

KEY NUMBER ONE
Listen

"Develop the inner vision and habit of listening to the inner Voice; and you are assured of unshakeable Peace and infinite joy."

– Atharva Veda

Ms. Z. E.

Oh no! she thought when the doors to the church opened and the smiling faces of 300 people looked back at her. *I don't know if I can do this!*

She stopped in her tracks, taking in every detail of the fairytale wedding she had dreamed about since childhood: the perfect gown, the perfect hair, the perfect bouquet, the perfect colors, the perfect matrons of honor and bridesmaids, and of course the cutest, most perfect ring bearer and flower girl. Everything was perfect. Well, almost everything.

She began to cry uncontrollably—her father on her left and her mother on her right, waiting to escort her down the aisle to marry a man she knew was not perfect for her.

I don't want to marry him. This isn't right... but it's too late.

She ignored the voice coming from within—the one that had been telling her for months (eighteen months, to be exact) that while this man was a nice guy and "marriage material," he was not "the one." Her crying had begun the day before at the wedding rehearsal, continued that night as she fell asleep, resumed at the church just before walking down the aisle, and persisted throughout the wedding ceremony and intermittently during the perfect wedding reception with more than 500 guests.

Before you can even hope to effectively communicate with other people, you must first be a master at communicating with yourself. But how?

The most important aspect of effective communication is active listening. Unfortunately, the majority of communication classes and books do not address what I call *intrapersonal listening*—listening to your inner voice. Some may also call this your higher self, God's voice, intuition, the universe, etc. While what you choose to call it is *not* important to this conversation, what is significant is that when you ignore it, things go awry. For the sake of simplicity, I will use the term *inner voice*.

How could Ms. Z. E. go through with a life-changing event such as marriage when her inner voice was telling her not to do so? You might ask this question if you have never done something you knew was wrong for you, or because maybe you have but it was not something as extreme as getting married. The simple answer to this question is: She did it because she was in the habit of ignoring her inner voice. It was a behavior that had been practiced for an extended period of time and so became a habit. Some of us pick up this habit when we are children.

Ms. D. I.

On a warm summer day, when she was about nine or ten years old, Ms. D. I. was playing with a boy from her neighborhood. He was about her age and someone with whom she had played many times, and their families knew each other well.

"You wanna go for a ride?" he asked her, sitting on his Little Rascals-style motorbike.

Oh yeah! That is probably fun! she thought as she nodded her head affirmatively.

"Here, hop on." He showed her how to sit on the back part of the bike's seat, and once she was ready, he mounted the bike in front of her. "Hold onto me so you don't fall off."

Butterflies fluttered nervously in her stomach as she followed his instructions. She had never been this close to a boy who wasn't a relative. *I hope he doesn't feel my hands shaking.*

Suddenly, he turned the ignition key and the bike rumbled to life. She watched carefully as he moved his right hand around the handlebar, making the machine jolt forward. They were moving! Riding on the motorbike was much bumpier than what she experienced riding her banana seat bicycle. As he drove them around the neighborhood, the butterflies settled and she relaxed as she felt the warm breeze caress her face and sweep her hair behind her. Time passed quickly and soon he stopped the bike and suggested that she drive.

What?!? I don't know how to drive!

He must've been able to read her mind, and quickly answered her objection, "I'll sit behind you and help."

After he dismounted the bike, she scooted forward on the seat into the driver's position and gripped the handlebars. Immediately, he placed his hands over hers and explained how to start the machine, how to make it move forward, and how to stop.

Seems easy enough. The butterflies in her stomach resumed their nervous flight while she breathed deeply and turned the key to start the machine. She jumped slightly at the sound of the motor and the boy laughed. She too laughed and, at his prompt, carefully turned the throttle to coax the bike forward. They traveled up and down the road several times before he moved his hands off of hers and onto her waist. Her confidence in her newly acquired driving skills was quickly replaced by discomfort and disbelief when his hands moved from her waist to the top of her thighs, then in between her legs, and up to her "private" area.

What is he doing? Stop! Stop! Stop! She screamed inside her head, but no words came out. She could not find the words as she struggled to push back the bile that was now burning her throat. When she saw a bump coming, she managed to say, "You better hold my waist. A bump is coming."

Her words fell on deaf ears as he kept his hands where they were and moved his fingers back and forth and up and down. Fearing she would wreck the motor bike if she tried to move his hands with one of hers, she kept both hands on the handlebars until she reached her driveway. With clenched jaw and eyes fighting back tears, she finally stopped the bike, jumped off, and found her voice. "I don't want to ride with you anymore," she said without looking at him. Without another word, she ran home.

Fast forward about three or four years…

It was a typical cartoon-filled Saturday morning, when Ms. D. I. bounced up from living room floor to answer the phone. She was about thirteen years old and despite being a young teen, loved being entertained by *School House Rock*. She hoped her mom would answer the phone but after the fourth ring, she looked away from the television to find her mom busy in the kitchen and ignoring the phone. When Ms. D. I. answered, an unfamiliar man's voice greeted her and asked for her by name. She politely stated that she was the person for whom he had asked. The man continued in a friendly yet authoritative voice with two questions: would she do him a favor and help him with a project and could she do so without anyone hearing her while she spoke on the phone? As she listened to his questions, she felt an uneasy sensation throughout her body and her stomach became unsettled. Something about his request didn't feel right to her and so she remained silent. When he received no response, he gently stated that she would be helping him out a great deal, that it would only take a few minutes, and that he would be very grateful for her help. Nervously, she found her words and stated that she needed to get permission from her mom before agreeing to help him. With a firm tone, the man quickly said that she was being bad by not agreeing to help him and that if she hung up on him, he would immediately call back and tell her mother what a disobedient child she was, which would likely get her in a lot of trouble. Believing him, and not wanting to him to get angry or call her mom, she agreed to help him. His voice became friendly once again as he instructed her to move the phone to where she would not be heard by anyone.

Uneasily, she peeked around the corner into the kitchen at her mom who was still busy and paying no attention to anything outside the kitchen. She then told him that she would need a second to move the phone and herself into the nearby coat closet. As she settled into the closet, she listened to him compliment her on being so grown up, so helpful, and so unlike other little girls he had asked to help him. His words did nothing to ease her discomfort. Once she was seated on the floor of the closet, she whispered that she was ready. He thanked her once again for her help and proceeded with telling her that he wanted her to repeat each word she heard him say immediately after saying it. She listened carefully as he started to read off a list of words: "butt, ass, penis, dick, vagina, pussy, c*nt…" Nausea introduced itself to her body as she heard each word and repeated them. It was like he was saying the words in slow motion because he seemed to take a long time to say them. She wasn't even sure what they all meant, but she knew they were words she had never heard from her parents and would probably get spanked or slapped for having said them if her parents ever found out about the "project." After each word, she heard the man breathe and moan loudly and congratulate her for doing such a good job. While the list of words was short, he stated them over and over again and instructed her to repeat them exactly as she was doing. After repeating them for seemingly dozens of times, she told him she couldn't help him anymore because she heard her mom coming and needed to hang up the phone. To her surprise, he said he understood, thanked her again for being such a good girl by helping him and ended the call.

Forcing down the taste of acid that rose to her throat from her stomach during the call, she took a deep breath, carefully opened the closet door, peeked out to see if anyone was there, and noticing that the coast was clear, exited and returned the phone to its usual home on the phone stand.

Until the day she told me, Ms. D. I. said she had never told anyone about what happened on the motorbike or on the phone. Though once she started sharing the first incident, she said she felt the floodgates open and felt compelled to keep going with the second. When I asked why she thought she had ignored her inner voice both times, she went on to say that somewhere in her early childhood she had learned that standing up for herself to anyone, especially a male, would only get her into trouble. She feared that if she told her parents, they would physically punish her for not being "good" or not asking for permission to ride the motorbike in the first place or for talking to a stranger and saying *bad* words. Thus, she dismissed her inner voice often and, in both cases, allowed her so-called neighborhood friend to violate her personal space and her body and a stranger to invade her mental sanctuary.

As you reflect on Ms. D. I.'s experiences, you may question whether it is possible to have had sufficient time to develop the habit of ignoring your inner voice at such early ages. After all, a habit is formed after it has been practiced for an extended period of time. Sadly, there is no need to analyze. The reality is that the habit had formed and consequences followed.

Perhaps it is more accurate to say that listening to our inner voice is common, but that *following through* on the guidance of the inner voice is where the real challenge exists. The inner voice is speaking and, though it may be heard, it is not given the attention it deserves; nor is it common for young people, unless they are exposed to holistic wellness programs, to learn to read bodily sensations as inner guidance, an important dimension of intrapersonal listening. According to Ms. D. I., she stopped intrapersonal listening before the age of nine. Based on the numerous experiences women have shared with me over the years while attending my personal and professional development classes, I conclude that a myriad, perhaps even the majority of women, also began developing their habit of ignoring their inner voice at a *very* early age.

Now, if my last statement is true for you, allow me to stop your mind from going down the path of "it is too late for me." This is absolutely *not* the end of the road. It is never too late to learn how to intrapersonally listen and give attention to what you hear. The first step is awareness and a decision that you want to increase awareness of your inner voice.

Reflection: When was the first time you can remember ignoring your inner voice?

Please be aware that as you begin to listen and give attention to your inner voice, you will have competition for your attention. The presence of your old habit will work to convince you to go back and listen to *it* instead. I liken this to characters on television or in movies who are facing a battle between good and evil and are often shown with two miniature versions of themselves, one sitting on each shoulder, the good dressed in white and the bad dressed in black. It takes practice to become aware of which voice is your true inner voice and which one(s) is/are not. Many times, the ones that are not your true inner voice are representing fear, insecurities, or other people's voices. Only you will know which one is your true inner voice. Reflect on past experiences to help you identify what it sounds like and how you felt when you heard it. Chances are high that when you listened to the true voice, the outcomes were positive and you felt a sense of peace.

The other aspect of listening is *interpersonal listening*. This is what is typically addressed in communication classes and books. Interpersonal listening occurs when someone else is speaking to you. Unfortunately, not enough attention is paid to the different levels of interpersonal listening, and listening itself often only gets cursory mentions in discussions about interpersonal communication. Not to worry, I have your back. You are about to receive a more comprehensive approach to interpersonal communication (you speaking to someone) with particular emphasis on interpersonal listening (when someone is speaking to you).

Let us now go two steps further with both aspects by breaking them down into the following: verbal and nonverbal listening and verbal and nonverbal speaking.

First, verbal and nonverbal *listening*. I once heard someone say that listening is the most important aspect of effective communication and that it ought to follow our biology. Meaning, since we have two ears and one mouth, it is best to listen twice as much as we talk. I agree with this recommendation and offer the same suggestion to you as you develop your ability to speak your mind without losing it. Listening attentively to other people serves as a foundational skill that enables you to be strategic with the words you choose to speak. Note though, there is a difference between hearing and listening. *Hearing* is simply the ability or act of perceiving sound vibrations by the ear. It is mechanical and, provided you are not hearing-impaired, it happens unconsciously or passively. *Listening*, on the other hand, requires conscious attention to receive the sounds perceived by the ear so that your brain may then process, analyze, and interpret the sounds. Listening is active whereas hearing is passive.

VERBAL LISTENING
WORDS

Verbal listening is listening to the actual words being spoken. That is easy, right? Not so fast. Many participants in my seminars have expressed that listening to the words is often a challenge because they get distracted by *how* a person is talking. I hear comments like, "Crista, if only my co-worker didn't sound so unprofessional when he talks to me, I would be able to work better with him," or, "Crista, when my spouse yells, I don't want to listen to anything he/she has to say." Do either of these experiences sound familiar? Notice what is similar between them. They are both opinions that have more to do with *how* a person has spoken rather than *what* the person has said.

TONE

Despite the challenge of being distracted by how a person is speaking, it is important to "listen between the words." In other words, listen for what is *not* being said in addition to the actual words. The trick is to do this strategically. Pay attention to the *how* just enough to draw an initial conclusion of the overall tone of the message or the emotions of the talker. Yes, I know. This is often easier said than done, right? It will, of course, take awareness and practice. Until you develop both, simply making the conscious choice that you are going to avoid being distracted by *how* the person is talking is enough to get you going on the right track. Do your best to set this intention before you start any conversation: "When I listen to my _____'s words, I am able to listen without being distracted by how s/he is talking."

> Reflection: When was the last time you can remember tuning out while listening to someone who was talking to you? Of what were you thinking when this happened?

NON-VERBAL LISTENING

Paying attention to someone's tone of voice is both verbal and nonverbal listening. What then is strictly nonverbal? The nonverbal part is what you *see* while the person is talking. Perhaps you are questioning how what you see has to do with listening? While you are not technically listening with your eyes, you are receiving sensory input that can help you understand what the talker is saying. Because messages that involve emotions and attitudes are often the most difficult to process, it is important to pay attention to the words being said, the tone with which they are spoken, *and* the body language displayed.

Non-emotional messages would be those that involve sharing data, facts, instructions, etc. If you have ever taken even just one communication class, you have likely heard of Albert Mehrabian, Professor Emeritus of Psychology, UCLA, and his "7%-38%-55% Rule" for the relational effect of words, tone of voice, and body language when communicating. Simply put, Mehrabian concludes that a message is most effectively expressed when the words, tone, and body language are consistent with each other. On the other hand, if there is inconsistency in the tone and the body language when compared with the words, the listener will pay more attention to the nonverbal aspects of tone and body language to interpret the message. For example, if I say to you, "Thank you for this beautiful necklace," and

I am smiling and have an upbeat tone, it is safe to conclude that I am happy about your gift. If on the other hand, I say, "Thank you for this beautiful necklace," while rolling my eyes up into my head, sighing, and exuding a disappointed tone, you will likely conclude that I am not happy about your gift even though my words said that I am.

ENGAGE ALL OF YOUR SENSES

In addition to paying attention to body language, I recommend noting other visual information. Details like how the person is dressed and their posture may help you determine how to best respond to what they are saying. A person who is carelessly dressed, has dark circles under their eyes, and stands with difficulty may deliver a message in a way that could give the impression that they are aloof or indifferent. Combine these cues with tone and words, and you may more accurately conclude that this person is exhausted and find it easier to respond with more compassion than judgment.

It can also be helpful to use your sense of smell and, as appropriate, your sense of touch along with your senses of sight and hearing.

When I was a supervisor for a telecommunications company, I had an employee who showed up late for work. Upon his arrival, he apologized, stated that he would make up the time on the weekend, walked slowly to his work station, and logged into his computer. I approached him a few minutes later to provide his stats from the previous day and noticed that he was sitting slumped in his chair, looking exhausted. When I asked him if he was okay, he responded that he was, but I noticed an overly sweet odor on his breath. His tone, posture, and breath communicated something different than his words, so I sent him to go see the wellness nurse. A few moments later, the nurse called and informed me that he was going to keep the employee in his office and possibly call emergency services because he suspected the employee may be experiencing diabetic ketoacidosis. Of course this is an extreme example, but my point is, do your best to be a detective when you are listening to someone by using all of your senses.

When you approach your interactions with a desire to obtain a complete picture of the message being sent to you, you increase your chances of being able to respond effectively. Taking in information in this manner will also help activate your left brain—the rational or logical part—that helps to balance the right brain, which houses emotions and creativity. If you have ever felt emotionally off-balance when listening and talking with someone, it is likely that your left brain was taking a break and your right brain was doing all the work. Do your best to get both sides working together.

MINDSET

Now, if you are like a lot of my clients, you may be feeling like these recommendations seem like a lot of work and that you just want to listen, respond, and get back to your day. Initially, these recommendations *will* feel like a lot of work. As with becoming proficient with any new skill, the ability to listen both verbally and nonverbally will take time, effort, and commitment. Since you are reading this book, I am going to conclude that you want to be able to successfully speak your mind without losing it because you are currently unable to do so. If that's true, then do your best to shift your mindset from perceiving what you are learning as *work* to a mindset that sees this information as the opportunity to become a better you!

Your mindset is your most powerful tool. Start to reshape it so that it works in your favor rather than against you.

STEP ONE: IDENTIFY YOUR DESIRED OUTCOME, ATTITUDE, AND BEHAVIORS

For example, before you interact with someone, first identify how you want the situation to end. Meaning, what outcome do you want? Then, figure out the effective attitudes and behaviors you must take into your interaction. Yes, you read correctly: *Identify what your attitudes and behaviors must be to support the outcome you desire.* Whether you realize it or not, the energy you carry with you into an interaction greatly impacts how the interaction will go. If you have a negative attitude and negative behaviors associated with a particular person, it is likely that you will automatically take these with you into your interactions with this person. It is a common mistake. If your desire is for an improved outcome, you must decide to choose more positive attitudes and behaviors *in advance.*

STEP TWO: PRACTICE EMPOWERING SELF-TALK

Now that you have identified the attitudes and behaviors you need to encourage the outcome you want, identify what you will tell yourself to ensure you project them. Taking this step is essentially programming your inner voice with what will best serve you in the actual situation. This is an important and necessary step.

Remember, you are likely reading this book because you have not allowed yourself to listen and follow your inner voice. As a result, when you do hear it during challenging situations, you probably question it and dismiss it because it is a habit to do so. The past is the past. It does not matter what you did or did not do in the past. What matters is what you do in the present and in the future.

When you come up with what you need to hear from your voice, you are bringing into your awareness what your inner voice would actually say. Because you are doing this in advance of the actual situation, you are calm and composed and not dealing with the potential stress of figuring out what your pep talk needs to be while in the presence of the challenging person.

A practical way to hone the message of your inner voice *before* a communication is to use affirmations. Affirmations are potent lines of empowering self-talk that build confidence in your ability to vocalize your inner voice. For example, you might repeat to yourself statements like: "*I am fully prepared for this communication*" or "*My heart knows what to say and my voice knows how to say it.*" Affirmations build trust and confidence in your inner voice.

There is no difference between this and what athletes do to prepare for competition. Athletes determine the mindset they need to take into a competition. Athletes practice the behaviors they need to possess to be successful in the competition. Those who make it to professional levels are well-aware of what it takes to keep them at the top of their game. Experienced athletes practice affirmations before a game such as, "*I am playing at my best, I am prepared for any situation, and my body knows what to do.*" Those who choose not to be committed to the effective mindset and consistent practice remain amateurs.

You are an athlete in your own game of communication. How will you play?

KEY NUMBER ONE:
Listen

☑ Intrapersonal listening = listening to your inner voice.

☑ Interpersonal listening = listening to other people.

- It is both verbal and nonverbal.
- Use all your senses to fully listen and receive a complete picture of what another person is communicating to you. The more information you have, the better prepared you are to respond effectively.

☑ Remember, your mindset sets the stage for your desired outcome.

☑ Choose attitudes, behaviors, and self-talk that support your desired outcome.

KEY NUMBER TWO
Project Confidence

"Being confident and believing in your own self-worth is necessary to achieving your potential."

—Sheryl Sandberg

Ms. V. A.
It was early August and the first day of school. The smell of the freshly waxed floors filled the crowed hallway as Ms. V. A. stood outside of her classroom and greeted the students, parents, and staff walking by her. She maintained a bright smile to hide her nerves as she processed the new sounds, sights, and unknowns of this first day of a new adventure. After many years working in the private sector, she was venturing into new territory as a middle school teacher in a public school.

Many parents stopped to introduce themselves and their children to her before moving on to their final destinations in her classroom or others. She appreciated how friendly they all seemed to be, especially when she noticed that many were the parents of students who were not going to be in her class. The warm welcome was helping to calm her nerves.

Finally after about eight or nine introductions, one of the parents asked, "What happened to the principal?"

"Excuse me?" Ms. V.A. asked, not understanding why she was being asked such a question.

"Well, I'm happy to be meeting *you*, but what happened to the last principal who was here for several years?"

"Oh! I'm not the principal. I'm a new teacher."

Just then, the actual principal approached them. She greeted the parent whose children had been students there for the previous two years, smiled at Ms. V. A., and moved on.

"Why did you think I was the principal?" Ms. V. A. asked the parent.

"Well, I guess I assumed that you were in charge because of how professionally you're dressed."

First impressions matter. Whether you like it or not, you and I and most everyone else on earth get first impressions based on physical appearance. When I facilitate courses on delivering exceptional customer service, one of the first points I make is that it takes only seven seconds for a person to form eleven impressions about you and your company or organization. Based on these eleven impressions, a person will make one of three decisions: to like you, to dislike you, or to be indifferent to you. And, as the 1966 ad for Botany Suits once expressed, "You never get a second chance to make a first impression."

People who are truly confident communicate it nonverbally from the inside out. This is why listening to your inner voice is so important and is the number one key. Presuming that you are well on your way to mastering *Key Number One: Listen,* here are ways to project confidence on the outside.

DRESS

Let us begin with how you dress. Someone once told me to dress for the job I want, not the job I have. Even if you are not looking to change jobs or careers, your overall appearance still deserves attention. Consider the saying, "a picture is worth a thousand words." What words do you want others to use to describe you? You are a walking billboard, shouting a message to the masses with what you wear. If you aspire to be the next vice president, choose clothing that declares, "Ms. Vice President." If you are a realtor and want million-dollar clients, make sure your wardrobe communicates that you represent million-dollar clients. If you want to be taken seriously the next time you present an idea to your church group, dress like you are going to church, not like you are about to clean it. Adjust what you wear to the outcome you want to achieve and the environment in which you will be communicating.

What if you are on a tight budget and can't afford to spend a lot of money on expensive clothes? That is a valid concern for which there is an easy fix. Take your current wardrobe to the next level with simple, low-cost fixes such as adding starch to your ironing routine or button covers to plain shirts, blouses, and jackets. It is not necessary to spend a million to look like it. Shopping at thrift stores located in the more affluent parts of your city is a budget-conscious way to dress for success.

Another benefit to dressing your best is its impact on your inner self. When you look good, you feel good. When you feel good, you send out positive vibes instead of negative ones. The positive energy you feel gets communicated when you speak and when you are silent. Even your resting face exudes a smile when you are not technically smiling. When you do actually smile, it is a smile that is genuine and includes your eyes. Your face sends a message before you say one word. Now, if you are smile-challenged and you find it difficult to smile even when you are feeling and looking good, invest one hundred pennies at your local dollar store for a mirror. Carry it with you and practice smiling often. Yes. I am serious. Go buy a mirror! Smiling people are often perceived as more intelligent and trustworthy. People promote, pay attention to, and hire those they feel they can trust, so practice smiling!

BE INTERESTED

Be interested and listen more than you speak. Notice I did not write *be interesting*. Your ego has no place in a world where you want to authentically convey confidence. Remember the tip from *Key Number One: Listen*? Listen according to your biology—two ears and one mouth. Listen twice as much as you speak. When you demonstrate interest in someone else by actively listening, you increase your chances of them listening and being interested in you.

Listening with your eyes comes into play here as well in two ways. First, as I explained in the previous chapter, pay attention to the visual information the speaker is giving you. Second, maintain appropriate eye contact with them. Since most people tend to have eyes that connect, disconnect, and reconnect with listeners when they are talking, it is best to keep your eyes on the face of the person to whom you are listening. If looking people directly in the eyes is not comfortable for you, consider looking at one of their eyes versus both or at the spot between their eyes. If you are more than two or three arms lengths away from the person talking, looking at their forehead, cheeks, chin, or nose may still give the impression that you are making eye contact. If you are speaking to someone from a different ethnic culture, do some research to find out what is considered appropriate for eye contact. For example, growing up in a multicultural state like New Mexico, I learned that Native Americans do not typically look people directly in the eyes. A Native friend explained to me that in her culture, the eyes are the windows to the soul and only certain people from her tribe had the right or privilege to take in that view. While living abroad as an exchange student in Yokohama, I noticed that the Japanese people did not use the same type of direct eye contact with each other as I used with other Americans. It is impossible to know all the do's and do not's. As such, do your best to do the best you can.

POSTURE

Check your posture. While it is not necessary to have the posture of a prima ballerina, it is important to stand tall with your shoulders back and your head held high. No, not high to the extent that you are looking at the ceiling. High to the extent that your chin is parallel with the floor, so you are not looking down. If you are not sure whether your posture is strong and erect, contact a local chiropractor, yoga instructor, personal trainer, or speech or voice coach, and inquire about a consultation. I have had many clients do this and they have received great feedback and even free recommendations of stretches and exercises to improve posture.

Strong posture helps improve the visual message you are sending, and it also helps you when you are speaking and need sufficient breath support for the words you want to say. Maintain this posture even when you are not talking with anyone. As you walk from place to place throughout your day, choose to walk with a purpose. The moments between your interactions are as important as the interactions themselves. They are times when you can listen to your inner voice for guidance. Take each step with confidence and gratitude that your presence in the world is a blessing. After all, it is!

What you do with your body has a direct impact on how you feel on the inside and how you are perceived by others. In her 2012 TED Talk, "Your Body Shapes Who You Are," Amy Cuddy, Ph. D., shares her research on "power posing," now called "postural feedback," and how holding wide, spread-out postures has a positive impact on how other people perceive you. Perhaps even more importantly, she explains that such expansive poses like that of

Wonder Woman help people feel more powerful and positive about themselves, which leads to an improvement in their mood and behavior as well. While, some of her peers criticized her initial findings, her paper published on March 2, 2018, in *Psychological Science* supports her original findings. The recommendation is to hold an expansive pose for two minutes prior to entering a situation in which how you will be perceived is important—like facing your kids in the morning. All kidding aside, such situations like a job interview or public speaking event are wonderful circumstances in which to practice these poses and project more confidence.

Ms. N. E.

The small lobby was full of actors from different agencies, waiting for their opportunity to audition for the director of the television episode scheduled to shoot the following week. Despite the number of people, the lobby was virtually silent as everyone did their best to respect the "Quiet Please — Casting Session in Progress" sign that hung on the audition room door.

I'm so excited... and nervous!

It was early in the New Year and Ms. N. E. had already had four auditions: three for television series and one for a feature film. This was the first call back of the year and she was happy about this audition. The role: scrub nurse.

A few minutes after the latest actor exited the audition room, the casting assistant opened the door and informed Ms. N. E. that she was next. With the lobby area now standing room only, she decided to give up her chair so someone else could sit. With a deep yet imperceptible breath, she rose from the chair and stood in the middle of the lobby.

Oh yeah, I could do a power pose. That will probably help me with these nerves...

Remembering a TED Talk she watched on power posing, she raised her hands to her hips, pushed her shoulders back, and lifted her chin for her best Wonder Woman stance.

I must look ridiculous, like I'm getting ready to take on a villain in my baby blue scrubs. Eh, I don't care.

She silently rehearsed her lines in her head, while in power pose, until she was called into the audition room. The door finally opened. It was her turn.

Before the casting assistant could finish introducing Ms. N. E. to the director and his two assistants, he said to everyone in the room, "Now *she* looks like a scrub nurse. She looks like she could run the operating room."

Feeling positive at the great feedback, she stood on her mark and, on cue, delivered her lines. The director asked her to give another read, which she did. Then he smiled and thanked her.

Have you noticed anything interesting thus far about *Key Number Two*? Like how I haven't made any recommendations for what to do to *sound* confident?

Because people are going to form impressions about you before you open your mouth, it is important to address those items before getting into what you will say and how you will say it. I also remind you to be sure you are using verbal and nonverbal listening so that when you do speak, you have obtained sufficient information about the speaker and what they have said to respond effectively.

Now, it is time to talk about *how* to project confidence with your voice. Let us then move into the Three Ps of projecting confidence: Pitch. Power. Pace.

YOUR VOICE: PITCH

Pitch is the degree of highness or lowness of a tone. For our purposes here, this pertains to the highness or lowness of your voice. Generally speaking, women have higher voice pitches than men. Speaking in the middle range of high and low is a safe place to be. The question then is: How do you know what your middle range is? Since we all have different voices, we all have a different middle range. Here is how you can determine yours.

Think about something exciting that has happened to you, or that you would like to happen to you. For example, you got a surprise promotion, won a vacation, won the lottery, found a lost family treasure, dropped a dress size, etc. How did, or would, your voice sound as you shared this exciting news? Generally, when we women are very happy and excited about something, our pitch goes up. The same can be true when we are very angry, but let us stick with positive-sounding higher pitches. Note this pitch as your high. Now think of how you feel when you are disappointed, extremely tired, sad, etc. These feelings tend to bring us down, not only physically and emotionally, but verbally in terms of pitch. How you sound when feeling these emotions would be your low. Now that you have your high and your low determined, what is in the middle? It is likely your everyday, business-as-usual speaking voice. If you think that your pitch is too high or too low, get the opinion of a speech or voice coach. This person can provide recommendations for how to make adjustments to get your voice sounding like you want it to sound.

Keep in mind though, that how you sound to yourself is different than how you sound to other people. To get an idea of how you sound to others, record yourself and play back the recording. When you play it back, you may determine your pitch is fine. However, most of my seminar participants and clients often state that when they do this, they do not like the sound of their voice in general and have difficulty focusing on just the pitch. There is no need to get consumed or nitpicky about the pitch of your voice. Simply being aware that it can have an impact on the message you are wanting to communicate is a good place to start.

YOUR VOICE: POWER

Power is about the forcefulness or strength of your voice. This includes clarity, volume, and strategy.

Clarity

This first aspect of Power is specific to whether you pronounce your words well enough to be understood. I have encountered both women and men who have power in their voice as far as volume and strategy, but lack clarity, which made them difficult to understand. Pronouncing words completely and correctly improves power. If you are not sure how to correctly pronounce a word, look it up online and click the appropriate button to hear the word. Granted, depending on where you live, there will be a lot of variety to how words are pronounced. This is an area for concern if you often receive feedback from people that they cannot understand what you are saying or they ask you to repeat yourself. When this happens, consider whether you are speaking clearly from a pronunciation standpoint.

I am reminded of the time I was presenting a seminar in Tupelo, Mississippi. I was teaching about words to avoid because they weaken your message. (Not to worry, I share these words with you in the next chapter.) The word I said was *try*. Yes, t-r-y. *Try*. My pronunciation was such that it rhymed with tie, bye, lie, and sty. The first time I said it, several participants asked me to repeat it. I said it again the same way and still more participants asked me to repeat it. Finally after repeating myself at least four times, I decided to spell it. Once I did this, the entire class stated in unison, "Oh, *tra!*" Their pronunciation rhymed with la, ma, bra, and saw. We all had a good laugh after I finally said the word "correctly" with their southern pronunciation and everyone finally understood what I was "tra-in" to say.

Volume

The next aspect of Power is the volume of your voice. Adjust the volume to fit the situation. Be aware that volume can unconsciously increase and/or decrease depending on the emotions you feel while you are talking. Also consider that louder is not always better when you are wanting to get someone's attention or make an important point.

During the opening session of a conference for metropolitan court employees, I delivered a forty-five minute keynote speech on how to move from overwhelm to action in high-stress situations. About midway through the speech, I lowered my voice to make that point that sometimes when someone is using a loud voice, responding to them with the opposite volume can be an effective way to get the conversation back on track. As I did this, I saw nearly every one of the 300 people in the room lean forward. Even though I was using a microphone and there was surround sound, the audience leaned toward me. When I reflected this change in their body position to them, they turned to look at each other and laughed when they realized what they had done. My point was made. After the session, many came up to me and shared that they appreciated the recommendation of lowering their voice instead of raising it when they want to get through to someone they perceive is not listening to them. They said that it would be a lot less stressful and help them feel more in control.

Strategy

The final aspect of Power is strategy. Strategy involves word choice along with clarity and volume. As I stated in the Introduction, my personal interactions were lacking when compared with my public ones, primarily because I did not prepare in advance. Of course the preparation for everyday interactions is not as detailed or extensive as what I do for public interactions, but the basic principles are the same.

The first step to being strategic is identifying your desired outcome. If you suspect that you have read this already, you are correct. It is one of the last points I made in the previous chapter. Identifying your desired outcome is always going to be your first step to speaking your mind. It is your opportunity to inform your brain of what you want to happen. This does not guarantee that it will happen, though it does start you on the right track. Remember, you are the athlete in this game of communication—the pros visualize winning, amateurs do not.

Once you have determined your desired outcome, consider the setting in which you are going to have the interaction. Will it be a private office with a door, or an open cubicle? Will other people be around? Is it a scheduled appointment or a break room "drive by"? How do you feel about the topic? What level of priority is the subject? How do you feel about the person with whom you will be talking? There may be more questions to consider and answer but for now, use these to get started.

Your answers help you identify words that may have greater impact than others, as well as where you may pause or add emphasis with humor, a gesture, an increase or decrease in volume, etc. As you are thinking about what you might say, be sure to avoid inadvertently weakening your message with credibility-stealing phrases like, "kind of/kinda," "sort of/sorta," "to be honest with you," and "to tell you the truth." The first two imply that you lack confidence in what you are saying. The second two are simply unnecessary. If you are actually speaking honestly, which I hope you are, there is no need to introduce your words with a prepositional phrase that says you are being honest.

YOUR VOICE: PACE

The third P is Pace. Pace is about how quickly or slowly you are speaking. As with volume, pacing communicates different meanings with the words you are using. How fast is fast? And, how slow is slow? Good questions. The average English-speaking American engaged in a casual and friendly conversation speaks approximately 110 to 150 per minute. Using a recording of myself from a keynote presentation I delivered for a conference of administrative professionals, I discovered that my average was between 140 and 170 words per minute. When I am speaking as host of my radio show, my pace is closer to the 170 mark. The average rate of speech for a television news anchor is between 150 and 175 words per minute. On the faster end of the spectrum, a professional auctioneer speaks between 250 and 400 words per minute. If you sense that you are losing the attention of your listener, consider adjusting your pace. Signs you may notice include the listener beginning to yawn, look away, fidget, look at their watch, etc.

Keep in mind that if you are wanting to improve your results when communicating to a group of people, the general ideas of what I have just shared do apply. There are more aspects to consider and additional recommendations based on the number of people, your goals, their goals, the setting, how well you know them, your role in relation to theirs, etc.—all of which are best saved for my next book. In the meantime, use what you are learning here as it pertains to speaking with one person at a time.

KEY NUMBER TWO:
Project Confidence

☑ Your appearance communicates a message before you speak a single word.

☑ Be *interested*.

☑ Use the Three Ps (Pitch, Power, and Pace) to help you project confidence and to help you understand how to most effectively communicate with another person.

☑ It is not *what* you say (words), it is *how* you say it (tone and body language). Make sure you are aware of all aspects of your message.

KEY NUMBER THREE
Keep It Simple

"Speak clearly, if you speak at all;
carve every word before you let it fall."

— Oliver Wendell Holmes

Ms. B. Z.

Whew! I just made it! she thought to herself as she scanned her boarding pass. She had requested to go standby on an earlier flight to Dallas, and it had worked out. But just barely.

Pulling her carry-on bag behind her, she made her way down the jet bridge to board the plane where the flight attendant met her with bad news: There was no room left in the cabin for luggage and her carry-on bag would be taken to the belly of the plane and delivered to her plane-side upon arrival in Dallas.

I thought this might happen. Well, I've done it before without a problem, she assured herself as she got her baggage-claim tag from the flight attendant and boarded the plane.

When she arrived in Dallas, she waited at the plane with the other passengers who had also had their baggage stowed at the last minute. One by one, each passenger received their baggage and went on their way.

Ummm... where is mine?

Puzzled, she asked a flight attendant where her carry-on was and, without answering, the flight attendant directed her to talk with the gate agent. Ms. B. Z. quickly made her way up the jet bridge and explained her dilemma to the gate agent.

After checking on the computer, the young and smiley agent frowned and said, "I'm sorry. Your carry-on never made it on the plane. It is still at the airport, but it can be placed on the next flight and delivered to you later tonight."

Frustration and disappointment were quickly replaced with hope. That is, until her luggage was not delivered later that night, the next morning, or the next afternoon. It was finally delivered to her approximately thirty-six hours after she arrived in Dallas. After multiple phone calls to the airline, here is how the final call played out the night before she was reunited with her baggage.

"I am calling regarding my missing carry-on."

"Have you called us previously?" The agent's voice was kind.

"Yes, I have called previously. Last night at 8:45 p.m. when I did not receive it as promised. I also called at 7:00 a.m. this morning as well as at 12:00 p.m., 2:15 p.m., and 4:45 p.m. today. It is now 6:00 p.m. and I have yet to receive my baggage, or an explanation as to why I have not received it, or when I will receive it. When may I expect to receive my carry-on?"

"We will get it to you as soon as possible, ma'am," the agent assured her.

"As soon as possible does not provide me with a time. Please note in my record that I want to be reimbursed for everything I have purchased as a result of being without my baggage since last night. I appreciate that the airline's policy only allows for reimbursement of up to $75 or 250 frequent flyer miles. That is not acceptable. I am here on business. My travel clothes are not appropriate for work. I have been without my toiletries, cosmetics, clean underwear, professional clothing, and dress shoes for more than twenty-four hours. As a result, I have purchased these items and the total cost is $300.59. I would like to speak with a manager about being reimbursed for all of my expenses as well as receiving frequent flyer miles."

With that, she paused and waited for the manager.

Simplicity is about creating and delivering messages that are easily understood by your audience. And yes, your audience can and often does consist of just one person. To help with simplicity, also aim for creating and communicating messages that are specific and accurate. The easiest way I have found to have all three of these aspects in a message is by learning to *avoid* certain words.

Earlier, I explained the Three Ps associated with projecting confidence. One of them, Power, addressed pronunciation and I shared the story of how the word *try* and my non-southern pronunciation of it left a memorable impression in Tupelo, Mississippi. Here is where you learn why *try* and other words are best avoided when you want to speak your mind effectively.

Try. *Merriam-Webster's Dictionary* defines *try* this way: "to make an attempt." Great! That clears things up, right? Wrong! While the intention is to communicate that an attempt is being made, the way the word *try* is often used is as a scapegoat to avoid commitment. For example, a family member calls and asks for your help with a garage sale next month. He has provided advance notice in hopes that you will be available. You are, in fact, available but you do not want to spend your weekend helping with a garage sale. Instead of communicating a simple, specific, and accurate message of, "Thanks for thinking of me. I won't be up for helping out," you respond with, "Thanks for thinking of me, I'll *try* to make it." Then when the time comes for the garage sale and you do not show up, it is easy for you to simply say that you never said you would be there, but that you said you would *try* to be there. Okay, so perhaps you would not have an issue with turning down this request. Good. Now, think for a moment about times when you have used the word *try*. Be honest. Were they times when you did not want to commit to something?

Try renders a message weak because it is does not satisfy the guidelines of simple, accurate, specific.

Before I continue, I want to go back and provide more explanation for what I mean when I recommend that your messages be simple, accurate, and specific.

Simple

When a message is simple, it means that the words are easily understood. I have delivered a myriad of classes to people in technical jobs: engineers, accounting, medicine, manufacturing, military, etc. Simplicity is one of the points I emphasize to participants from these industries because there can be a tendency to communicate with a lot of industry-specific language. This is fine when the communication happens among people with similar backgrounds and job descriptions. It is *not* so fine when those similarities are limited or completely absent. For example, an engineer who is communicating with a military representative, who is not an engineer yet, is the project manager for the current six-month initiative. While they often share common ground with the initiative itself, they often do not share each other's industry-specific vocabulary that is filled with jargon, abbreviations, codes, and acronyms. As a result, keeping things simple is key. Achieving simplicity may mean spelling things out and/or providing examples to ensure information is understood by all parties involved.

Accurate

Referring back to the handy-dandy dictionary, *accurate* is defined as: "1. Free from error. 2. Conforming exactly to truth or to a standard."

When communicating, are you eliminating errors and are you being truthful? I recognize that the question may appear to be a bit complex or even perfectionistic. However, the reality is that it is important to be truthful when you are speaking your mind with the goal of not losing it. You may hear your inner voice give you feedback when you are not communicating with accuracy. Perhaps you are thinking the same thoughts that my seminar participants have expressed regarding the use of white lies or fudging the truth depending on the situation. This is not meant to be a discussion on accuracy or truth to that extent. If you decide that it is helpful to explore this specific area further, please do so. When I share the other words to avoid, the examples I provide are sure to bring more clarity. As a result, you may conclude that accuracy is basically about being straightforward and direct.

Specific

Defined as "free from uncertainty." Is the report due at two o'clock or *around* two o'clock? Do you want help with organizing the volunteers, or do you *sort of* want help organizing the volunteers? Being specific is similar to being accurate. They both support simplicity and the three provide a checks-and-balances approach to creating powerful messages. I am breaking down messages to this level of detail so that if you choose to self-evaluate, you have tools to quickly and easily make the necessary adjustments.

Now, back to the words to avoid.

Don't: As you read the following description, do your best to picture it your mind. You are in a grassy park. You are seated beneath a large tree. To your right, you see children playing in a playground. To your left, you see adults playing chess. Directly in front, you see a ladybug on a blade of grass. Don't see a pink elephant crossing the street. Above you, an airplane flies by.

Tell the truth. Did you see a pink elephant crossing the street? I did too. Our brain works in such a way that it can only process *dos* rather than *do nots*. Even though I wrote "don't see a pink elephant crossing the street," the mind had to see it first and then un-see it to follow the *not* or *n't* of the word do. Once seen, the pink elephant cannot be unseen. The word *don't*, when used in messages, fails on all three points regarding simplicity, accuracy, and specificity.

Consider the following scenarios:

1) A friend calls you and invites you to go to lunch for your birthday. She says that you may pick any place you want. After a few seconds of

allowing you to think about where you want to go, she asks if you have a place in mind. You respond by saying, "I don't want to go to Lily's Place because they're always packed. I don't want Asian since I had that yesterday. I don't like noodles so that new place is out…"

2) One of your direct reports has called in sick. There is a presentation at the end of the day with which he was going to assist you. You contact his peer and inform her that she will be taking his place during the presentation since she was the designated backup. When you meet to go over the final notes, your review goes something like, "Don't forget to make an extra copy of the slides… Don't seat the off-site supervisor next to the door… Don't turn on the projector until everyone is seated…"

I know. You never express yourself with so many *don'ts*. Really? How about simple statements like

"Don't forget to throw out the trash," "Don't call me at 10 a.m. during the staff meeting," "Don't slam the door."? Are you still innocent? Me either, though I use *don't* a lot less often today than I did fifteen years ago.

To be simple, accurate, and specific, say what you really want to say to get the outcomes you want. With the lunch invitation, simply answer the question and identify where you DO want to go. With the work scenario, take out the don'ts and you have "remember to make an extra copy of the slides… Seat the off-site supervisor next to the window… Please wait to turn on the projector until everyone is seated…"

A final point about *don't*. When used, it places the responsibility of your message on the person to whom you are talking because you have not provided a clear alternative. Something as simple as "don't slam the door" is a weak message. "Oh, but Crista, it means to close the door gently." Well, what if the talker wanted the door left open or ajar? How is the listener of the message to know for certain what the talker actually wants? Mind reading does not work, nor does assuming. Therefore, remove *don't* from your vocabulary and don't use it ever again. Ha! And, avoid using it ever again. There. That is better.

But / However. When either of these words are used, there is a tendency for the listener to stop listening because they anticipate that whatever follows will be bad news. For example, "I would love to help you with the project but I am already booked," Or, "You did great on the fundraising campaign, however you missed the goal." The listener may also receive a mixed and confusing message. In the second example, the word *however* negates the positive feedback.

Participants in classes have often defended the use of the words *but* and *however*, stating that sometimes real life is about giving and receiving bad news or constructive feedback. Yes. This is true. Consider though what your desired outcome is when you are talking with someone. On the most basic level, your goal is to have your message received. If avoiding the words *but* and *however* increases your chances of getting your desired outcome, then it is worth the effort to reword your message in favor of your goal.

Could / Can. These words are often used inaccurately, especially when making requests. When you are unsure whether a person has the ability to do something, ask the question using the word *could* or *can*. When you are certain of a person's ability to do something, then you are inquiring about willingness. In this case, the request is stated with *would* or *will* instead of *could* or *can*. At this point, I typically get some looks of confusion from workshop participants, especially the women.

If you are familiar with the work of John Gray, Ph. D., you know that he has authored many books on the subject of male-female communication. His best-known books are the *Men Are from Mars, Women Are from Venus* titles. The words *could* and *can* fall into this arena pertaining to differences in communication between men and women. Here is how I processed what I learned from reading several of Dr. Gray's books. On Venus, Venetians use twice as many words as Martians to communicate. They are also very helpful to one another. When a Venetian makes a request of another Venetian by stating, "Could you call this vendor for me?" and she receives a yes response, she knows that the call will be made. Over on Mars, things are different. On Mars, a Martian would never ask another Martian if he *can or could* do something. To do so would be asking what is, in their mind, a question to which every other Martian knows the answer, which is always "Yes." This is because Martians can do EVERYTHING. Because Martians know this about each other, the words *could* and *can* cease from existing as options for words Martians use to make requests. They use *would* and *will* because they are inquiring about another Martian's willingness.

When a Martian visits Venus and receives the "Could you call this vendor?" request, the Martian immediately says, "Yes." Two hours later, after the Venetian has not received the call back from the vendor that she is expecting, she approaches the Martian and asks whether the phone call was made. "No," is the Martian's response. Confused, the Venetian asks why the call was not made. The Martian explains that she did not ask him to make the call, she asked him if he *could* (was able to) make the call, not whether he *would* (was willing to) make the call.

I know. I know. There are exceptions to this scenario. The bottom line is: Choose the words that most accurately communicate your message. In the case of *could* and *can*, when you know a person has the ability, whether woman or man, make your request using *would* or *will*.

Should. The word *should* weakens a message because it is vague. It implies rather than clearly states. It is often used retroactively to express an expectation that was not communicated from the onset. Here are some examples of how *should* is often used: "You should have notified me that the meeting was starting late." "The board of directors should have an answer to me by morning." "He should run those numbers a third time." Now for examples of stronger messages: "The next time the meeting is starting late, please notify me." "I expect the board of directors to have an answer to me by morning." "I recommend that he run the numbers a third time."

Wish. Similar to the word *should*, the word *wish* is unclear. Some may choose to use the word *wish* instead of the word *want* for fear of being perceived as demanding. Please repeat after me: What other people think of me is none of my business.

Wish defined: "(verb) feel or express a strong desire or hope for something that is not easily attainable; want something that cannot or probably will not happen; (noun) a desire or hope for something to happen."

Notice the lack of strength of the word with its accompanying definitions. If you are stating that you wish for something and it is something that is not impossible, your word choice is inaccurate and not specific. You therefore run the risk of your message not being received well or taken seriously, neither of which are desirable outcomes.

Notice the difference between the statements that follow:

I wish I would get a raise.	I want a raise.
I wish you would do your work.	I expect you to do your work.
I wish I could have some candy.	I would like some candy.

Need. Let us take a trip down memory lane to that Psychology 101 class you took with 400 other people. Do you remember Maslow's Hierarchy of Needs? Of course you do. Just in case you have forgotten a few of the details, allow me to refresh your memory. There are five need areas: physiological, safety, love/belonging, esteem, and self-actualization. I recall these needs when I consider using the word *need* in my messages. Yes, I know. I do think a lot and analyze what I am going to say. While I do not expect this from you, I do advise that you think twice about using the word *need* and, when you do, whether you are using it accurately according to some or all of Maslow's Hierarchy. The reality is that most of what you may be saying is a need is actually a want. When that is the case and you use *need* instead, your message is not accurate or strong. Here are some examples with alternatives for your consideration:

I need this report by five o'clock.	I want/expect this report by five o'clock.
I need you to work late.	I would like you to work late.
I need your signature.	I require your signature.

True *need* statements: I need to pay my mortgage. I need to eat. I need to pee. I need to take my medication. I need to sleep.

Have to / Got to. Both of these phrases are not accurate. There is only one thing in life you and I *have to* do and that is die. It is a fact that everyone dies. No one has a choice in the matter as far as if it will happen. Therefore, using *have to* or *got to* are untrue when you use them to express any other idea. I refer to these phrases as victim language. They weaken your message because anyone can call you out on them and they would be correct to do so. Take the following common statements: "I have to go to work." No, that is untrue. "I have to pick up my kids." Nope. "I have to buy groceries." "I have to finish this book." "I have to go to church." "I have to get my Master's degree." "I have to pay my taxes…" All of these are your choice to do or not do. "Oh, but Crista, if I miss work, I'll get a write up. If

I leave my kids at school, the principal will get upset. If I am delinquent on my taxes, I could go to jail."

The fact that negative consequences exist if you make a particular choice does not eliminate the option to choose. Here, I will rework the phrases:

I have to go to work.	I get to go to work.
I have to pick up my kids.	I am going to pick up my kids.
I have to buy groceries.	I want to buy groceries.
I have to finish this book.	I want to finish this book.
I have to go to church.	I get to go to church.
I have to get my Master's degree.	I want to get my Master's degree.
I have to pay my taxes.	I choose to pay taxes.

Reflection: Which of these words do you recognize as being prominent in your everyday interactions? Choose the one you feel you use most often and plan for how you will avoid it in the future.

Now, let's revisit Ms. B. Z. Do you remember if she used any of the words from the avoid list? It's okay if you want to go back and peek at her story.

That's right. She avoided all of them. I imagine her experience as a frequent traveler helped her maintain her cool in this situation. Also note that she was highly specific with the information she shared and requested. She did not say she spent *about* $300.59. She did not say she *kind of* wanted to speak with a manager, that she *had to* buy new items, or even that the airline *should not* have left her baggage. Using any of those words or phrases would have weakened her message; and when you use them, they will weaken yours. So, promise me, and more importantly yourself, that you are going to stop using the words to avoid from this chapter as well as the phrases from the previous chapter.

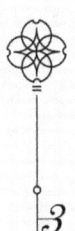

KEY NUMBER THREE:
Keep It Simple

☑ Create messages that are simple, specific, and accurate.

☑ Avoid these words:

- Try
- Don't
- But / However
- Could / Can
- Should
- Wish
- Need
- Have to
- Got to

☑ Venetians rule!

KEY NUMBER FOUR
Leverage the Power of "I"

"Be impeccable with your word. Speak with integrity... Use the power of your word in the direction of truth and love."

– Don Miguel Ruíz

Ms. I. L.
Her flight out of New York's La Guardia International Airport finally departed at 8:00 a.m., two hours after the original departure time; but after waking at 4:00 a.m. to get to the airport on time, Ms. I. L. did not care.

I just want to board the plane and go to sleep. She was scheduled to arrive in Las Vegas, Nevada, at

5:14 p.m., but with the delay, she had no idea what time she would arrive much less when she would get to her hotel.

After a long flight that included a two-hour layover in Denver, she finally arrived in Las Vegas, picked up her rental car, and drove to her hotel. Exhausted and hungry, she waited in line in the lavishly decorated lobby of the hotel/casino to check in. Despite being far away from the nearest casino entrance, the lobby reeked of cigarette smoke.

When it was finally her turn, she stepped up to the desk, promptly spoke her name, and handed the clerk her driver's license and credit card. She wanted this to go smoothly and quickly so she could get to her room, order some food from room service, eat, and go to sleep. After a long week working in New York City, and her body still on east coast time, she was ready to collapse even though local time was only 9:00 p.m.

I will be lucky to get enough sleep to avoid having bags under my eyes for the wedding tomorrow, she thought as she watched the clerk click away at the computer.

Unfortunately, as she daydreamed about her room service order and finally getting to sleep, the clerk, Hilda, brought her back to reality with the words, "I'm sorry, ma'am, but we are overbooked and the only room available is a smoking room. Will that work for you?"

Are you kidding me? Ms. I. L. wanted to cry and yell at the same time. She was worn-out and famished and now she might end up sleeping in a room that would make her sick.

Instead of crying or yelling, she took a silent deep breath and said, "There are only smoking rooms available. I see. No, that will not work for me. I acknowledge that the hotel is overbooked. I prepaid my reservation for a king-sized bed in a non-smoking room to ensure that I would not be bumped in the event of overbooking. I have severe allergies and, because I used to work in the hospitality industry, I know that smoking rooms are deodorized after guests leave. Even still, I am not willing to take the risk that I will get sick by sleeping in a room where smoking is allowed. I have had a very long day of travel to get here and I have my cousin's wedding to attend in the morning. I know that neither of these are of any concern to you. Still, I need your help. At this point, I do not care about the size of the bed. My priority is to sleep in a smoke-free room. Hilda, would you be so kind as to search your room inventory again for a non-smoking room?"

Hilda smiled at her and said, "Let me see what I can do."

What did you notice about how Ms. I. L. spoke to Hilda, the hotel clerk? If you noticed that she avoided the words that weaken messages, you are on the mark. She also used the most powerful word she could have used in any language—the clerk's name. If you are not currently in the habit of referring to people by their name, especially in situations where you are wanting to persuade or convince, start today. Using a person's name is a tip I make sure everyone uses in my classes on communicating with difficult people. This is not to say that Hilda was a difficult person. I am simply making the point that when you personalize your messages by referring to someone directly, your chances of being heard increase. The reason I make sure everyone focuses on this when communicating with difficult people is because when people are not anonymous, they tend to behave better. When you use their name, it sends a clear message that you know to whom you are talking and you may likely remember it in the future.

Back to what else Ms. I. L. did well. She expressed herself with simplicity, specificity, and accuracy. She spoke from a position of authority and projected confidence by using *I* instead of *you*.

Even though the word *you* was not included on the list of words to avoid, it is one to use with caution. A recommendation I consistently give in my classes is to use *I* before *you*. Structuring your messages in this way positions you to speak from the only place you have 100% ownership—yourself. It also prevents your messages from having a demanding tone and gives your messages and inner voice one of the Three Ps: Power. Take a look at the statements that follow as well as the suggested alternatives. Notice that the *you* statements contain words to avoid. The *I* statements are the remedy. Use them as a guide for turning any of your *you* statements into *I* statements.

You make me so mad.	I am mad.
You need to call me when the meeting ends.	Call me when the meeting ends.
You should be prepared.	I expect you to be prepared.
You have to leave at noon.	I recommend you leave at noon.
You made me forget my thought.	I forgot my thought.
You don't listen.	I am not feeling heard.

In addition to situations like the ones involving Ms. B. Z. in the previous chapter and Ms. I. L. at the beginning of this one, be sure to use *I* messages in all other situations and especially when you want to decline someone's request. Yes, there will be times when you want to decline what someone is asking, or perhaps mandating, you to do. How to Say No is a common subject in many of the classes I have designed and delivered for support staff. Of course, whether your job is that of a support professional or not, the main concepts apply:

a. Acknowledge the request
b. Decline the request / say no
c. Explain why - optional
d. Offer alternatives - optional

While the concepts are mostly straightforward in and of themselves, allow me to provide more information to ensure you are prepared to implement them. Feel free to see them as steps, though exact order is not necessary after the first step.

Acknowledge the request. An easy way to acknowledge is to repeat what you heard the speaker say. Starting off your acknowledgment with phrases like, "What I hear you saying is…," and "I heard you say…," is effective for helping you stick to repeating what you heard. Perhaps you have received the recommendation from other books or classes that an effective acknowledgment phrase is "I understand…" This is *not* a phrase I recommend. In fact, avoid this phrase. To say that you understand is inaccurate and therefore does not satisfy the guidelines I provided in the chapter for *Key Number Three: Keep it Simple*. Using this phrase can also backfire when used with a difficult person because they can accurately dismiss anything you say after "I understand" by saying that you do not understand. The reality is, no matter how empathetic you are doing your best to be, it is impossible for you to truly be in another person's shoes for any situation. We all respond to events and people differently. Okay, I will get off my soap box now about "I understand."

Decline the request / say no. Depending on the person you are responding to, what you say to decline will vary. Recall the Three Ps from earlier in the book. Are this person's Ps similar or different than your own? Do your best to model your "no statement" after the other person's Three Ps, especially their Power. Strong Power often means the person is a direct communicator and fewer words have a greater impact. For example, saying, "I am not available" will likely be sufficient to decline. Someone with moderate or low Power is likely more of an indirect communicator. As such, common courtesy statements like please and thank you are appreciated and help them truly listen to your message. For example, "Thank you for asking me. I am not available."

Explain why. I identified that this aspect is optional for an important reason. If your communication style has lower Power, it is going to be key that if you decide to explain why you are saying no, Keep It Short and Simple (KISS). This is particularly important when the person wanting you to do something has a high Power communication style. As I just mentioned, fewer words have greater impact. It is up to you to determine if you want to explain why you are declining. This is another area where there is a consistent difference between how women and men communicate. While I have not conducted an official scientific study on this notion, I have found through my observations of how people communicate that men explain themselves less than women do when making decisions, including when they say no to something.

Offer alternatives. As with explaining yourself, this aspect is optional. If you have options you think may be helpful, offer them. Be careful though that you are not offering someone else to attend an event or manage a task without their permission, or yourself at a later date when you really do not want to say yes at all. If saying yes for a later time, date, etc., is something you feel good about, then by all means offer that option. Nevertheless, I have found that this is not often the case, and women are simply leaving the door open for themselves to be talked into saying yes.

Perhaps you're thinking that you do not have a challenge with saying no but dealing with how you feel afterward. If you have ever felt guilty about saying no, please revisit *Key Number One: Listen*, where I indirectly addressed guilt and any other emotion you may experience that leads you to second-guess yourself. Again, when you are in sync with your inner voice, there is peace and confidence. Emotions like guilt, resentment, fear, shame, etc. no longer have a home in your world. Unfortunately, if these emotions have been present for a long time, it is going to take consistent practice of becoming aware of which voice is your inner voice and which is not. You can do it!

Ms. E. F.

It was a brisk Saturday morning in early March, and Ms. E. F. was at work. It was her day off, but she was in the office working on a special project that was above and beyond her regular responsibilities as a supervisor. The building buzzed with the activity of sales representatives, supervisors, and managers working to accomplish their first quarter goals. The smell of coffee filled the air as she heard an announcement over the intercom about the prize of the hour for the person with the most verified sales. Working Saturdays was an option for frontline employees while supervisors and managers had a rotating schedule.

Despite all of the noise in the building, Ms. E. F. was in the zone and getting a lot of work completed. Unfortunately, her productive rhythm was disturbed when a manager came to her cubicle and asked, "Could you work with one of the sales teams at 2 p.m.? The scheduled supervisor has not shown up for his shift, and we need someone to cover for him."

Ms. E. F. looked up from her computer and said, "Hi, Dave. Did I hear you correctly, that you would like me to work with one of the sales teams because the scheduled supervisor did not come to work?"

"Yes." Ms. E. F. smiled and confidently responded, "I see. I am in the middle of a project at the moment. I am not available to help out today."

"Oh, okay. I guess I'll go ahead and do double-duty and cover for the supervisor and make my rounds to the other teams. Thanks anyway."

Now that was easy, right? For some of you, yes. For others, no.

> **Reflection: If saying no in this situation would have been difficult for you, identify why this would have been the case.**
> **If saying no would have been easy for you, think of a situation where it would have been a challenge to say no and reflect on the difference between the situations.**

Many participants in my classes over the years have expressed that they can easily and confidently say no when at work, yet when at home or in personal situations, they become a "yes person." Ms. A. T. was one of those people.

Ms. A. T.

It was a few months before summer break and Ms. A. T. had gone home for the weekend from college to visit family and, like most college students, to stock up on food and do laundry. While there, she ran into a family friend at the store who asked Ms. A. T. what her plans were for the summer.

"I'm considering moving back home for the summer to work and save money for college."

"That's great. The bank where I work is going to be hiring tellers and I'd be happy to put in a good word for you if you want to apply for a summer position."

"Yes, that would be amazing. Thank you." She thought about how great it would be to work a job over the summer that possibly could lead to her getting a similar job in her college town once she returned to school in the fall. Enthusiastically, she informed her parents of her plans to move back home to work for the summer and they seemed on board with the idea.

The rest of the semester flew by and before she knew it, it was already the end of April. On another food-and-laundry trip home, Ms. A.T. reminded her parents that the semester was ending soon and that she would be home right after her last final exam, take a few days off, and then begin her job at the bank.

"Well, I would like you to apply for a job at the conference center. Working there would mean a shorter commute than working at the bank," her dad said matter-of-factly.

Disappointed at her dad's lack of support toward the bank job, she replied, "I have already been hired at the bank and I do not want to work at the conference center. Besides, all the available summer jobs are likely already filled at this point."

Her dad did not respond in the moment, but that evening, he handed her two pieces of paper stapled together. "Here is an application for the conference center," he said as he held them in front of her. "I went over there earlier and found out that they are still hiring and that you can still apply. They have positions open in housekeeping."

Blood beginning to boil, Ms. A.T. responded as calmly as she could, "I do not want to work at the conference center, especially in housekeeping. I have my heart set on working at the bank and believe that it will look great on my resume and give me experience that could get me a job later."

He stared at her, as if he didn't understand what she was saying. And, rather than continue to repeat herself, she took the application, quickly completed it, and left it on the kitchen table.

The next day, as she drove back to the university, she prayed her dad would support her decision to work at the bank and drop the idea of the conference center job. No such luck.

About a week later, she received a call from her dad. "You have been hired as a housekeeper at the conference center."

"How did that happen? I didn't turn in the application."

"Oh, I did that for you. And now you don't have to worry about spending so much of your money on gas to and from the bank job since the conference center is much closer."

Pressure formed in her chest as he spoke. She was an almost twenty-year-old adult and her father was making decisions for her as though she were still a child. She fought back tears of frustration as she opened her mouth to explain her intentions again. Despite the myriad of words and thoughts that raced through her mind, all she could muster was a sigh and, "I'll think about it."

Sitting in her dorm, she wondered, *Do I take the housekeeping job and get him off my back? Or, stick to what I want, keep the bank job, and have an entire summer hearing him tell me how I am wasting my money on gas to commute every day?*

She called the next day to ask her mom's advice and request that she help convince him to favor the bank job. The phone call was a waste of time. While her mom was in favor of the bank job, she said she may as well take the conference center job because her dad would simply remind her all summer of how much money she was wasting on gas.

"Fine. I'll accept the housekeeping job." The minute she said yes instead of no to her dad, she felt an ache in her gut and a small voice in her heart telling her to say no. Each day she worked that job, the voice in her head beat her up. Because the lodging rooms had no televisions or radios and she cleaned the rooms alone, she worked in silence—that is except for the voice in her head from her childhood schoolmates and relatives that told her she was fat and unattractive, and a new voice that said she was weak for giving in to what her dad wanted, that she would now not have a job worthy of resume placement and on and on. By the end of the summer, she had indeed saved more money by taking the housekeeping job than she would have with the bank job; but she also started her fall semester seeing a counselor to help her deal with the exercise bulimia she developed as a coping mechanism to silence the shouting negative voices in her head.

Reflection: What has saying yes when you wanted to say no cost you? Peace of mind, time, self-love, self-respect… what else?

Hindsight being 20/20, I bet there are plenty of times you would go back and say no when you said yes. Rather than beat yourself up as Ms. A. T. did, use those experiences as the strength you need to stick to your guns and say no. Your sanity and peace are worth it.

KEY NUMBER FOUR:
Leverage The Power of "I"

- ☑ Speak from a position of 100% ownership by using *I* before you use *you*.

- ☑ Use the most powerful word in any language—a person's name.

- ☑ Say yes only when it works for you.

- ☑ Say no with confidence.

    - Acknowledge the request
    - Decline the request / say no
    - Explain why - optional
    - Offer alternatives - optional

KEY NUMBER FIVE
Own It

"When you learn how much you're worth, you'll stop giving discounts."

— Karen Salmansohn

Ms. S. I.
Ugh, I don't want to be here, she thought as she looked around the lobby of the court-approved mediator. Three desks filled the waiting area whose walls were lined with green fabric-covered chairs and shelves full of non-fiction books. The magazines in the floor racks ranged from *National Geographic* to *Car and Driver*, none of which interested Ms. S. I. She would have preferred to be anywhere else that day, yet there

she was. The home owners association (HOA) was suing her for not paying an outstanding balance on her account and had placed a lien on her property. Fortunately, because the court's dockets were overflowing with other cases, the judge assigned the case to mediation as an option to resolve it out of court.

The mediator, a friendly, petite, fifty-something woman, with a wavy brunette bob hairstyle, greeted Ms. S. I. in the lobby and escorted her to the conference room where the representative from the HOA's management company was already seated. This woman also appeared to be in her late fifties, sporting a pixie-style haircut and long red-polished fingernails. The smell of a powdery air freshener filled the pale blue-green room, and a framed print of swans on a lake hung on the wall behind the HOA representative.

If this gets argumentative or emotional, I'm going to look at that to help me stay focused.

The mediator efficiently and professionally introduced herself to the women, the two women to each other, and then went over the format and guidelines for the mediation. When she was finished, she asked if either woman had a preference for speaking first or second. Ms. S. I. stated that she wanted to speak second.

In agreement with the order, the HOA representative matter-of-factly proceeded with her information, which was nothing more than repeating that which had been stated in the letters the lawyers had sent and in the lawsuit documents. The bottom line was that from their perspective, the outstanding balance must be paid within thirty days in order for the lien to be removed from the property and to avoid going to court.

When it was Ms. S. I.'s turn, she remained silent as she took out a neatly organized folder with copies of the lawsuit and attorney letters. She also placed a copy of the HOA's Declaration of Restrictions, Covenants, and Conditions in front of her before she looked up at the management company's representative and the mediator and said, "Thank you for your time."

She continued by removing an additional document from her folder—a copy of an account statement sent to her by the previous HOA management company that showed a zero balance. She provided both the mediator and HOA representative with a copy of the document to address the HOA's contention that an outstanding balance had carried over from the previous management company and it was this amount ($2,000+) that must be paid.

As a final point, Ms. S. I. read an excerpt from the HOA Declaration, which stated that prior to the board of directors issuing a delinquency assessment or taking legal action, they must give a homeowner at least thirty days' notice to attend a hearing to present their side of the situation. Then she said, "I was never given notice or an opportunity to attend a board of directors hearing and, because of this, the board is in violation of its own rules."

Eyes wide and mouth partially open, the management company's representative asked, "May I see the Declaration page?" Ms. S. I. provided her with a copy and after reading it for herself, her face turned a pale shade of red. "I never knew such a requirement existed and, off the record, the board has violated the Declaration and, in my opinion, your rights. I apologize and will contact the HOA's board of directors immediately."

"Thank you," Ms. S.I. responded smiling.

Whew! She sighed with relief as she gathered her papers and got up to leave the meeting.

As you read about Ms. S. I.'s experience, there were probably moments where you were wondering if she expressed that she was upset that she was being sued or that it was unfair, etc. She shared with me that she was upset and did feel the situation was unfair, yet she decided ahead of time that she was going to keep her composure and only relate the facts. Notice how she did some mental preparation before the mediation. This is something you can do before most situations you encounter. Now, let's talk about some specific ways to own your message and keep your composure at the same time.

If I were to ask people in your life whether you own what you say, what would be their response? For some of you, the response would be in your favor because when you speak, people take you seriously and clearly understand what you are saying. For others of you, the response would be the opposite because when you speak, you are not taken seriously and are difficult to understand. For the rest, the response would be a mix because sometimes you are effective and sometimes you are not. It is possible to move yourself from inconsistent to communicating effectively more often than not. That, of course, is the reason for this book. Specifically, this chapter focuses on yet another word to avoid and how to own all of your emotions. I begin with the word to avoid.

SORRY

Yes, I am sure you thought I had covered all of the words that weaken you messages back in the chapter on *Key Number Three: Keep It Simple*. I saved this one for now because it deserves special attention and its own chapter. The word is *sorry*. Unlike the other message-weakening words, *sorry* also includes a non-verbal aspect—an apologetic tone. First, the word itself. Referring again to my unscientific collection of data on how people communicate, *sorry* is a word that is frequently overused and used inaccurately.

When I have addressed this word in my classes, people often comment that they are not even aware they are saying the word at all or as often as they do. One place you may use it is when saying no, as a way to acknowledge what someone is saying. I often hear it in traditional customer service settings when the employee of a company is not able to follow through on a customer request, or as a way to acknowledge an inconvenient or unfortunate situation. For example, "I'm sorry I'm not available to work late today." Or "I'm sorry the wait in line was so long." While neither of these statements are horrible, they are weak.

Let us visit the dictionary for the definition of *sorry*. Sorry: "(adjective) feeling regret, guilt, sympathy, pity; regrettable or deplorable; unfortunate; tragic; sorrowful, grieved or sad." For the two statements above and/or any similar type of situations where such statements may be expressed, check whether the definition of *sorry* truly applies. One way to do this is to substitute *sorry* with any of the words used to define it. If you are like the majority of participants in my classes that I instruct to do this, replacing *sorry* with the other words creates an exaggerated sentiment that does not accurately express how they actually feel about the situation. Therefore, reserve the use of the word *sorry* for when you really do feel its true definition. For all other times when you want to express less profound sentiments or that you are simply apologetic, saying, "I apologize" or "My apologies regarding…" is sufficient.

Words of caution. Be sure that when you apologize, you are doing so for something that is actually *in* your control. Apologizing when the line to check out is long or when someone is out of the office or when it is raining outside, etc. will not serve you or others. Here are the alternatives:

Instead of Saying…	Say…
I'm sorry the line is long.	Thank you for your patience.
Sorry, she's not in the office.	She is not available. How may I help?
I'm sorry it's raining.	Thanks for your patience during the rain.

Reflection: Recall a time when you said sorry. Did you use it accurately? If not, what word could you use instead in the future?

The final point in the recap for *Key Number Two: Keep It Simple* stated that it is not *what* you say, it is *how* you say it. Be aware that even if you are not using the word *sorry*, your tone may sound apologetic. When this is the case, your message is weak and likely will not be received the way you want. Here is where getting feedback from someone else and/or recording your own voice can be helpful.

Begin to check whether you are owning your messages when you introduce yourself to other people. Consider that every interaction you have is an interview. Use the informal settings where you meet people to practice your skills. Prepare a fifteen- to thirty-second self-introduction for all occasions—in line at the grocery store, post office, bank, etc. The more you practice, the more confidence you will have when the pressure is on during executive visits to your office, the next board meeting, or that networking event. Help people remember you and your name by pausing for one or two seconds between clearly speaking your first name and your last name.

Now, on to the aspect of owning your emotions.

EMOTIONS

What I am referring to here are all the different types of circumstances in which you will be communicating. There will be times when you are right about something and the other person is wrong or vice versa. There will be times when you are angry, frustrated, upset, sad, happy, disappointed, nervous, excited, etc. There will be times when you are feeling exhausted, ugly, fabulous, hungry, gorgeous, etc. Because you are not a robot, you must account for all of the emotional aspects that make you who you are. Up to this point, you may have concluded that I was recommending that you lose the emotional elements of how you communicate. After all, I have provided a lot of "left-brained" types of suggestions for checking yourself and your messages. Those recommendations would not serve you well if I did not advise you on how to blend them with all of the wonderful emotion-based characteristics that make you, you.

The first step in blending the emotional aspects with the technical ones is to honor them. Honor ALL of your emotions. The 2015 American 3D computer-animated comedy-drama film produced by Pixar Animation Studios and released by Walt Disney Pictures, *Inside Out*, does a phenomenal job of illustrating how important all of our emotions are. While the movie does focus on the emotional growth of a girl from birth to preteen years, its themes are relevant for adults as well. The two main points that I gleaned from the movie that speak to the idea of honoring your emotions are that all emotions are essential in order to experience life to its fullest.

Simply put, without the "negative" emotions, it would be impossible to know and experience the "positive" ones. The second point is to avoid projecting your own emotions onto someone else by expecting them to feel as you do. This, of course, is right in line with using *I* messages to express yourself. When you speak from the position of *I*, you are owning your words and your emotions.

Therefore, blending the emotional with the technical is about speaking from the position where you have 100% authority and control—yourself. If this is not specific enough for you, revisit the Three Ps and how they typically show up when you are dealing with an emotionally charged situation. If you discover that the Three Ps you have used in the past have prevented you from your desired outcome, adjust them. While doing so, be sure that you are tuning into your inner voice for guidance.

If what you are hearing from your inner voice is riddled with emotions that will not serve you if you express them, spend whatever time you have available to honor them by listening to them without judgment. I do this by talking to them in second person. For example, "Crista, I am hearing a lot of anger, disappointment, fear, etc. You have the right to feel this way. You are not a bad person for feeling the way you do…" When I do this, I often end up feeling calmer and more emotionally balanced much sooner than when I used to attempt to ignore the feelings or force myself to feel something different. I am then able to come up with the words I need to best communicate. I am confident you will have a similar experience. It may seem strange to talk to yourself this way at first, yet discomfort is replaced by comfort with consistent practice.

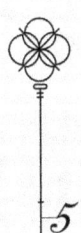

KEY NUMBER FIVE:
Own It

- ☑ Reserve use of the word *sorry*.

- ☑ When it's necessary to apologize, say "I apologize" or "My apologies for…"

- ☑ Remember that an apologetic tone can weaken your message as much as inaccurately saying *sorry*.

- ☑ Be prepared for all occasions with a fifteen- or thirty-second self-introduction.

- ☑ Honor ALL of your emotions.

KEY NUMBER SIX
Decide

"Begin with the end in mind."

– Stephen R. Covey

Ms. R. C.
Dear Ms. Clinic Director:
 I have mailed a check for $50.00 (check #1234) to bring my account with your clinic up to date. I greatly appreciate your patience. I sincerely apologize for any inconvenience the delay of payment has caused. While I respect your right to collect on a past-due balance, I want to take this opportunity to express my points of view with you about what I experienced when you brought your concern about the matter to my attention during my session on 9 January.

First, and with all due respect, I found your interruption of my session with my counselor, not only surprising but highly unprofessional. I am puzzled why you did not bring it to my attention either before or after my session. If this was such an important issue, why is it that the person with whom I scheduled the appointment did not refuse my appointment request? Why was my session allowed to not only be scheduled but started in the first place? There is clearly no policy pertaining to this type of situation, or if there is, training on such is lacking.

Second, my previous interactions with you, while limited, had always been cordial, respectful, and courteous, which is what I would expect from any other person and particularly someone who works in mental health. I was disturbed that your demeanor that day was anything but cordial, respectful, and courteous. I can appreciate that in matters concerning client responsibility, a firm tone of voice is sometimes necessary. Ms. Clinic Director, I found your tone to be harsh, condescending, and inappropriate. Had the past due amount been in the hundreds or thousands of dollars, I might have be able to accept the tone that I heard coming from you. For $50.00, I am unable to excuse it.

Third, I felt attacked and as if I was a criminal being interrogated when you demanded to know how I was getting food and paying for utilities. I was embarrassed as I felt compelled to reveal that I was receiving food assistance benefits from the state, had applied for utility assistance, and that I was two payments behind on my mortgage to justify why I had not been able to pay the $50.00 I owed to your clinic. My guess is that you had not thoroughly researched my account prior to confronting me because if you had, you would have known that my medical insurance coverage was being provided by Medicaid and not some expensive private insurance or even the moderately priced insurance I had prior to 1 July. I imagine this fact alone might have given you some rationale as to why I was behind on my payment. Or, perhaps not. Perhaps you did know and simply chose to accuse me, in tone, of attempting to evade my financial responsibility.

Fourth, as I have reflected on the interaction with you since that day, I have been doing my best to be empathetic and have even attempted to rationalize the behavior I witnessed and to which I was subjected. Perhaps you were frustrated that it was taking so long for me to pay. I too was frustrated that I was unable to pay. The thought also occurred to me that there may have been some gender or ethnic prejudice coming into play. With you being a Caucasian woman, I have wondered whether your tone and demeanor would have been the same if I was a man or Caucasian instead of a woman and non-Caucasian. I told one friend about my experience with you that day. Until I shared with him, not a single person knew the extent of my financial challenges. Not my counselor, not my parents, no one. I see these challenges as temporary as I work to rebuild my business after getting divorced, and I am taking full responsibility to restore what was once-stellar credit history and high self-worth.

While I will likely never have an explanation for your choices that day, I am doing my best to put the experience behind me or "just drop it" as my friend recommended. Now that I finally have the ability to pay my debt, I believe that I am one step closer to leaving this issue behind me—at least to a financial extent. Nevertheless, I do not believe that simply mailing you the check and saying nothing about what I experienced with you is the answer.

I have not determined whether I will use this letter as part of a formal complaint with State officials. If I do, I will give you the benefit of copying you on any correspondence I submit. My hope is that what I experienced on 9 January, is not how you typically handle situations such as mine and that no one else is subjected to anything similar in the future.

Sincerely,
Ms. R.C.

This is a letter a client wrote and shared with me. As you read it, did you get the sense that Keys One through Six were present? Yes, this is a trick question. I have yet to tell you about the sixth key, so how could you know if Ms. R. C. implemented it?

In previous chapters, I identified the importance of identifying your desired result before you interact with someone. Let's go one step further with this concept. I am going to presume the outcome you desire is one that is in your favor. Beyond this, what is the *purpose* of your message? **Decide** what it is. Is it to persuade, educate, request, mandate, inform, inspire, reprimand, reward, correct, etc.? To be a masterful Ms. Communicator, you must think past yourself to the other person for a moment. Your purpose may not be in line with what they expect to get from your message. When that is the case, your chances of achieving your desired outcome are minimal.

> **Reflection: Recall a time when someone communicated a message to you and they were not clear about what they wanted. How did you handle it?**

I often share in my seminars and keynote presentations the fact that nearly every person with whom we communicate has one question on their mind: *What's in it for me?* If we look at this question with only its initials it ends up sounding like a radio station: WIIFM. This question is not exclusive to the listener of our message; it is also relevant to you, the person sending the message. We are, therefore, all tuned into the same "station!" Recall for a moment any desired outcome you have identified and my previous presumption is proven to be true—you are seeking something you want. How then do you communicate to get what *you* want AND what the other person wants? For the answer to that question, I will share a brief lesson on negotiation, conflict management, and mediation skills.

While I was working toward my Bachelor's degrees in Communication and Spanish at the University of New Mexico, I became certified in mediation and conflict resolution. The most powerful thing I learned from that class was the importance of having a clear understanding of the *positions* and *interests* of all parties involved and giving higher priority to the interests rather than the positions. Of course, as a third-party mediator, that is expected. However, I have carried this insight into situations where I was one of the people involved in a communication or conflict.

If you have ever taken a mediation, negotiation, or conflict resolution class or read books on these subjects, you likely received an explanation about the difference between a *position* and an *interest*. For those of you who have not taken a class or read a book on either subject, this will get you up to speed.

A *position* is the desired outcome. For example, if one of your employees is requesting a day off from work, the day off is her position. Your position may be that you want her to work on the day she is requesting. Simply stated, the position is the "what."

An *interest* is the reason behind the position. Using the same example, the employee wants the day off because her daughter is leaving for college that day and she wants to see her before she leaves. Your reason for wanting the employee to work is that on that day, two vice presidents are visiting the company and you want her to give them a tour of the building and bring them up to speed with the company's progress on a new community initiative. The interest is the "why" behind the "what."

Ineffective communication and frustrations arise when the parties involved only identify and discuss *positions*. By identifying and discussing *interests*, you increase your chances of creating a *win-win* outcome instead of a game of tug-o'-war.

Other outcome options are also available, though they are not as effective as a win-win outcome. *Compromise* may be an outcome that you have been offered or have sought. Compromise results in a win-lose, lose-win situation. Meaning, you partially get what you want and so does the other person. Because it is a partial win, both you and the other person lose something to gain the partial win. Another option is to *compete*. When you compete for what you want, there is a winner and a loser. When you give in and give up your desired outcome, you are choosing to accommodate and create a lose-win outcome. Finally, you may decide to *avoid* the situation altogether. As you can see with the four options above, the outcomes are less desirable than working toward a win-win, also known as *collaboration*.

With this additional information, you are now better equipped to determine your overall desired outcome and consider how to approach and genuinely account for the other person's. When you decide the purpose for your message, it becomes easier to determine the words you will choose to speak your mind and ideally influence a win-win outcome.

Now that you know that the sixth key is Decide, you may have concluded that Ms. R.C.'s purpose was to inform, and that her desired outcome was to prevent anyone else from having an experience like hers. That is the same conclusion I drew. In terms of whether she followed Keys One through Six, you be the judge. This was not a quiz and so there are no right or wrong answers.

There are likely statements or ideas that you would express differently had you authored a similar letter. That is a good thing. As I mentioned previously, being an effective Ms. Communicator is not about sounding or writing like anyone other than yourself. Ideally, you will not have an experience like she did, but if you do, I recommend using the letter as a guide for how you might approach it so that you are adequately prepared to speak your mind without losing it.

KEY NUMBER SIX:
Decide

- ☑ Decide the purpose of your message. Possible options: persuade, educate, request, mandate, inform, inspire, reprimand, reward, correct, etc.

- ☑ Keep in mind the question on everyone's mind: What's In It For Me? (WIIFM)

- ☑ Make identifying and understanding the *interests* of both parties a higher priority than the *position*.

- ☑ Decide on *collaboration* for a win-win outcome.

KEY NUMBER SEVEN
Reflect and Celebrate

"Do not be conformed to this world, but be transformed by the renewal of your mind that by testing you may discern what is the will of God, what is good and acceptable and perfect."

— Romans 12:2

About a year after my run-in with Sharon at the big training, I was presenting a class on conflict management and confrontation skills to an audience of eighty women and men from various industries. People who attended this course typically fell into one of two categories: 1) people wanting to be there or "volunteers," and 2) people mandated to be there or "hostages." We were all packed into a hotel meeting room with low ceilings and poor lighting.

The first half of the class addressed the importance of owning one's attitudes and behaviors before focusing on how to deal effectively with someone else's. About an hour into the program, right after I had stressed the importance of having emotions in check before confronting someone, a short, forty-something, Yosemite Sam-looking man in a white button down shirt, faded jeans, and scuffed steel-toed boots, sprang up from his seat in the front row and started in on me: "Look here, little missy. This is a bunch of bullsh*t! If I do what you're saying and p*ssy-foot around everyone I deal with, lives will be in danger…" With each word, his face and his ears turned a brighter shade of red.

Dude, did you not have your coffee this morning? I sarcastically thought to myself while keeping one eye on him and the other on the rest of the participants as they sat silently, waiting for him to finish his monologue and anticipating my response.

This guy is obviously a "hostage" whose boss mandated him to attend this class, most likely to simply give some relief to his coworkers. I can tell he is not coachable and no matter what I say, he is going to find an excuse to discredit it. I'll just let him continue his rant until I hear the signal that it is my turn.

I remained cool as a cucumber, standing with my arms at my side, in my navy blue pants suit and hair in a neat, curly up-do fit for a meeting with the governor or any other executive. When I heard him begin to repeat himself, it was my cue to take back the room.

Not having learned his name, I noticed a company name on the front of his shirt. Looking him squarely in the eyes, I proceeded to use it as his name to get his attention and interrupt him, "Mr. ABC Energy Company," I clearly and loudly stated so that everyone in the room could hear. "I appreciate your perspective. Today's class is about providing you and everyone else with options that are proven to be effective. Based on the fact that you are here today, I presume that either you or your employer, my guess is your employer, decided that how you are currently communicating is not working. Use the recommendations or not. It is your choice. I do expect though, if you decide to share your opinions during the rest of the class, that you raise your hand and wait for me to call on you before speaking."

As soon as I finished speaking, he forcefully grabbed his jacket from the back of his chair, and with face and ears even redder and smoke seemingly exiting his nostrils, he spewed, "This is a bunch of bullsh*t and a waste of my time! I'm outta here!" Then he clumsily maneuvered behind the seats of the ten other participants seated between him and the closest exit.

As soon as he was out of the room, the audience erupted with applause, cheers, and whistles. I smiled back at them, enjoying the sweet reward of not only speaking my mind without losing it, but modeling it for the room.

It is now time for you to have specific ways to reward yourself for your determination. Let's begin with a "congratulations" to you for making it to the seventh key! I hope you're excited about becoming a masterful Ms. Communicator. This final key ties all the previous keys together and helps ensure that every time you implement them, you are continuing to fine-tune and increase your effectiveness when communicating.

Throughout the book, I have presented you with **Reflections** and questions, generic scenarios, and actual stories. As I shared in the Introduction, these components are meant to help bring to life my recommendations by encouraging you to think about your own situations and how you may go on to improve your own skills. One of the points I made early in the book was "that which gets rewarded, gets repeated." Another way to look at this is that you are more likely to repeat a positive behavior when you reward yourself by acknowledging your success. The gold medal athlete surely recalls what she did to win the race as much as how it felt to be rewarded afterwards for her efforts. Both are important aspects of consistent success.

Perhaps you are wondering why rewarding your efforts is so important that it gets its own chapter. First, have you noticed that generally speaking, we women do not often celebrate our successes?

If you do celebrate, that is great. Most do not. This is likely because many of us were brought up with the belief that "tooting our own horn" was "unladylike" or "unbecoming." There may have even been the proposition that if you work hard enough, you will get recognized without having to ask for it or draw attention to yourself. Unfortunately, it is true that the squeaky wheel does get the oil, and the silent one stays rusty and stuck. Now, I am not by any means suggesting that you suddenly become some boastful and in-your-face type of person whose only mission in life is to be celebrated and recognized. Quite the contrary. While celebrating your successes with improving your communication effectiveness may likely transfer to external circumstances, the goal with *Key Number Seven: Reflect and Celebrate* is to strengthen your inner voice with positive feedback.

Reflection: What has your inner voice been saying to you as you have read this book?

If I were to take a guess, I would say that you have been hearing a variety of messages from your inner voice. This is normal and expected. Remember, your voice has likely been suppressed for a long time and overpowered by the voices of fear, insecurities, other people, etc. It is possible that you are still working to determine what your true inner voice actually sounds like. To help you identify it and support it, begin by keeping a journal. Your journal may be handwritten, electronically typed, or even voice recorded. Choose whatever works for you. Make note of your thoughts and how you feel both physically and emotionally with those thoughts. Doing this simple exercise helps you reconnect with yourself by increasing your intrapersonal awareness. As you develop the habit of documenting in this way, you can advance to collecting notes on your interactions with other people. These notes will be less about the other person and more about how you responded to them and what your inner voice was telling you during the interactions. Your journal is where you may begin to celebrate and reward yourself. For example, at the end of each day, visit your journal and highlight, place a star, or otherwise decorate anything that you want to celebrate. Initially, you may simply be rewarding yourself for entering one item. Make this a daily practice, and eventually it will become a habit.

Here's what a sample journal entry may look like:

> Today, when I received my lunch order and it was not prepared as I requested, I used the food truck worker's name, thanked him for his friendly service and reminded him that I had ordered my tacos without cilantro. Before I could ask for them to be remade, he smiled and apologized and said that he'd have fresh ones made quickly and offered me a free bottle of water while I waited. Yes! In the past I would've just eaten the tacos and gagged on the cilantro. Yay, me!! 😀♡

Aside from your journaling, celebrate by doing things you enjoy. The more you reward your efforts, the more effortless they become.

KEY NUMBER SEVEN:
Reflect and Celebrate

☑ Identify specific ways to reward yourself every time you speak your mind without losing it.

☑ That which gets rewarded, gets repeated.

☑ Strengthen your inner voice with positive feedback.

☑ Reconnect with yourself and increase your intrapersonal awareness by journaling.

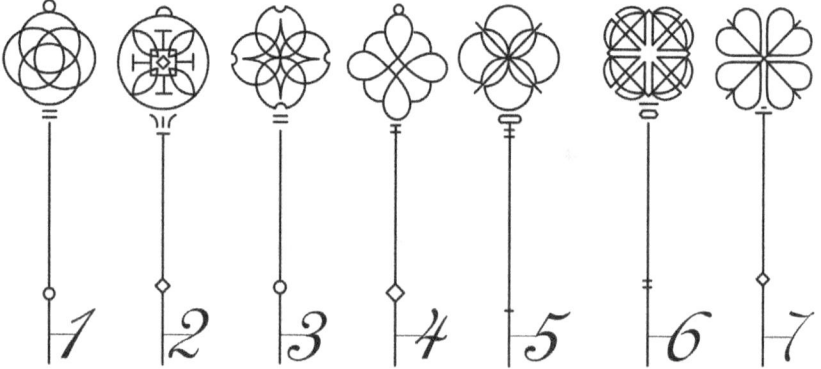

CONCLUSION
Communication Can Be Complex Because We Are

"To be yourself in a world that is constantly trying to make you something else is the greatest accomplishment."

— Ralph Waldo Emerson

The Seven Keys to Speak Your Mind Without Losing It are guides. The client stories are examples of successes as well as lessons learned. Have you been wondering what happened to the clients whose stories I shared? Wonder no longer. To quote one of my favorite storytellers, Paul Harvey, "And now, the rest of the story."

Ms.

Remember Ms. Z. E., the reluctant bride who didn't listen to her inner voice? A year after getting married, she was transported to the hospital by ambulance with chest pains and difficulty breathing. After numerous tests, she was diagnosed with viral pericarditis. While she was given a medical reason for the symptoms and was referred to a cardiologist for a month of post-diagnosis care, she knew deep inside that she was suffering from a broken heart for having gone through with the marriage she knew was not right for her.

A year after the diagnosis, and after attending a church retreat for newly married couples, individual counseling, and couples' counseling, she realized she could no longer continue being married and told her husband she wanted a divorce.

Seven years later, after a five-week courtship and three-month engagement, she walked down the aisle again. And again, she was crying. She thought that because they both wanted a family, this commonality was sufficient for moving ahead with marriage.

Almost another seven years, and two children later, husband #2 asked her if she was happy and told her that if she wasn't, they may as well get divorced because he was tired of being treated like sh*t.

Unable to answer him in that moment, she said that she would take some time during her upcoming business trip to reflect on his question and answer him when she returned. Sitting in her hotel room later that week, alone, she asked herself, *How, once again, have I allowed myself to be in an unhappy and unfulfilling marriage?*

As soon as she asked the question, she remembered the night it had all gone wrong.

They had not planned to get engaged so soon after beginning to date, but their original plan to live together first had changed suddenly at a family dinner hosted to inform her parents of the cohabitation plans. By the end of that dinner, the conversation had turned to marriage.

Ms. Z. E. remembered hearing a still, small voice in her, *Say no. This is premature. Stick to your plan.*

Unfortunately, she was unable to fight the second, louder voice in her head that said, *No, just be quiet and don't embarrass him in front of your family by correcting him.*

And I still had so much opportunity to change my mind. She recalled that after dinner, they had driven to a spot overlooking the city and taken a walk. The cool November air filled her lungs as she breathed and replayed what had just happened at dinner. On the walk to the lookout point, he shared how he had prayed for a woman like her and that God had blessed him with her; and before she knew it, they had stopped walking and he was down on one knee proposing.

Again, the two voices returned. One was weak yet pleading: *This isn't supposed to be happening yet.*

The other louder, more convincing voice shouted, *Don't embarrass him. This is so romantic. Don't hurt his feelings by saying something stupid like you need to think about it or just no altogether.*

The second voice won and she said yes.

Ugh, why didn't I listen to that voice? she asked herself, staring out the hotel room window at the twinkling lights of the city. *I'm not happy. I have to tell him.*

Upon return from her business trip, she informed him that she was not happy and wasn't sure whether the marriage would survive. They agreed to seek assistance from a counselor, even though they had already been working with a counselor for the previous two years and had attended a church program for married couples. Four months later, after separating from each other on alternating weekends so that their children would remain in the comfort of their home, Ms. Z. E. agreed with her spouse's previous statement that divorce was the right choice. While he disagreed and initially fought it, two months later, the dissolution of marriage was finalized.

Alas, the true inner voice was heard, but only after seven years in a second marriage that was never what she really wanted. She is grateful for the blessings of her two children and while she never dreamed of raising them in a 50/50 shared custody arrangement, she knows in her heart that the peace and happiness she regained after the divorce will serve her children far more than staying in an unhealthy marriage.

Remember Ms. D. I.? Now an adult with these incidents in her past, she expressed that she no longer wanted to keep them a secret. Until she gave me permission to share them here, I never shared them with any of my audiences. It seems they were meant for this book as examples, all be they extreme, of the trauma that can result from dismissing the inner voice's guidance. Ms. D. I.'s goal as a mother of two children is to teach them to honor their feelings/inner voice by speaking them, feeling them, and trusting them with the hope of helping her children avoid the years of guilt, shame, and fear she has finally been able to release as she approaches half a century of life.

Ms. V. A. is no longer a middle school teacher, though she cherishes the connections she made with the parents, students, teachers, and administrators during her two-year tenure at the school. While education and educating others is still her passion, she prefers working with adults and continues to do so as a consultant with companies and organizations representing various industries.

Ms. N. E. is now a member of the Screen Actors Guild after booking the role that day and three others after it. She has no delusions of grandeur about becoming the next "overnight" success, though she is open to whatever opportunities may present themselves as she continues to put her best foot (and power pose) forward on every audition she accepts.

Ms. B. Z. no longer travels to the extent she did during the time her luggage was left behind, but she did walk away from the incident with all of her expenses reimbursed and 2,000 frequent flyer miles.

Ms. I. L. is happy she stood her ground about wanting the non-smoking room because she received a double upgrade to a two-bedroom suite and a voucher for breakfast the next morning—in the non-smoking section, of course!

Ms. E. F. no longer works at the company though she did maintain a positive relationship with the manager. She also completed the special project, which was adopted company-wide.

Ms. A. T. is fully recovered from exercise bulimia and now uses exercise and food in a constructive way by participating in online fitness challenges. The most important part of her recovery was not fully realized until nearly ten years later, when she was able to forgive her parents for their lack of support and give them the benefit of the doubt that they were doing the best they could to advise her.

Ms. S. I. received a date for a hearing with the HOA's board of directors during which they determined they had no evidence to prove the outstanding balance was her responsibility and agreed to drop the lawsuit and remove the lien from her property.

Ms. R. C. never mailed the letter and remains undecided about whether she will. She does, however, feel accomplished with the fact that she wrote it.

These women all had powerful experiences around communication, and it's not hard to see how their choices in their communication (or lack of it) resulted in big challenges or big rewards. Which women did you most relate to throughout the book?

I'll tell you who I related to the most: All of them. And I'll tell you why.

Look closely at all the initials beginning with Ms. R. C.'s. Now, beginning with the C and working backwards, place the letters together. What do you get?

CRISTA FELIZ BENAVÍDEZ.

I am the Ms. Communicator. I experienced all of these situations.

My sister Ms. Communicators and honorary Mr. Communicators, we are not two-dimensional, one- or two-story beings. We are complex, simple, experienced, wounded, naïve, strong, determined, injured, recovering, intelligent, emotional, logical, passionate…people! The real key to speaking your mind without losing it is to draw on your past experiences—ALL of them—learn from them, and use them as fuel to propel you forward.

Always remember that the most important relationship you can have with a person is the one you have with yourself. Love it. Cherish it. Celebrate it. Honor it.

About the Author

Crista F. Benavídez's public speaking experience began more than thirty years ago when she ran for President of her school's junior high Student Council and won. She went on to win more competitions and attend the University of New Mexico, where she earned Bachelor's degrees in Communication and Spanish and a Master's Degree with Distinction in Organizational Learning and Instructional Technology.

After acquiring experience in food service, hospitality, and telecommunications, Crista ventured into the world of entrepreneurship in 2000 by founding Cristalk International, LLC, now named Chispas Performance Solutions.

Today, Crista is an internationally recognized speaker specializing in interpersonal communication, a.k.a. "soft skills," and organizational learning. She has over twenty years of experience, presenting nearly 2,000 programs, working with groups from a variety of industries with clients such as Texas Instruments–Mexico, United States Forest Service, 150th NM Air National Guard, IBM, University of New Mexico, CISA, and many others. Her areas of expertise include effective leadership, behavior/communication styles, customer service, communicating with difficult people, effective teaming, and more.

Crista's high-quality professional training helps businesses and organizations combat ineffective communication and the unnecessary interpersonal and financial costs that inevitably result from it. She is described by audiences as engaging, dynamic, and highly motivational.

She lives in Albuquerque, New Mexico, with her two children, is a member of the Screen Actors' Guild (SAG/AFTRA), and shares tips for improving communication on her weekly radio show, *Biz Day New Mexico*, which promotes New Mexico-registered businesses and organizations.

Take Action!

Ready to share your communication successes and or lessons learned? Many people who have participated in my programs have shared with me their communication stories and I often pass them on, with permission of course, in my classes and presentations. If you too want to share, consider submitting a description of your story so that others might learn from your experience by way of my programs or the next book in the *Ms. Communication* Series. For information, visit MsCommunicationBook.com.

Finally, if you are inclined to leave a review where you purchased this book and on any social media websites where you participate, your invaluable feedback will help us shape the next edition.

www.MsCommunicationBook.com

Publisher's Note

Thank you for reading *Ms. Communication: Seven Keys to Speak Your Mind Without Losing It!* Please pass the torch of connection by helping other readers find this book. Here are some suggestions for your consideration:

- Write an online customer review
- Gift this book to friends, family, and colleagues
- Share a photo of yourself with the book on social media and tag #mscommunication
- Bring in Crista F. Benavídez as a speaker for your business, club, or organization
- Suggest *Ms. Communication* to your local book club, and download the Book Club Discussion Questions from CitrinePublishing.com/bookclubs
- For bulk orders of 10 copies or more, contact Citrine Publishing at (828) 585-7030 or email Orders@CitrinePublishing.com
- Submit a story and connect with the editor by visiting MsCommunicationBook.com/stories

Contact Chispas Performance Solutions today to book Crista for your next event!

Keynote Speeches

Breakout Sessions

Corporate On-site Sessions
(one-hour, half day, full day, and multi-day designs)

All programs are available in English, Spanish, and bilingual formats.

For more information, contact
info@ChispasPerformanceSolutions.com.

www.ChispasPerformanceSolutions.com

www.ingramcontent.com/pod-product-compliance
Lightning Source LLC
Chambersburg PA
CBHW052132110526
44591CB00012B/1696